WHEN FEAR AND FAITH COLLIDE

WHEN FEAR AND FAITH COLLIDE

7 STRATEGIES TO UNLOCK YOUR GOD-GIVEN POTENTIAL

DR. NIC WILLIAMS

WHEN FEAR AND FAITH COLLIDE

7 Strategies to Unlock Your God-Given Potential

ISBN   978-1-61961-422-2   *Paperback*

978-1-61961-423-9   *Ebook*

. . . .

To my parents who always said I could be whatever I wanted and supported everything I have ever tried…even if I was bad at it. Although they would never tell me if I was bad at it. Thank you for your love and support.

To my brother who has been my friend since I was born. Just remember, they picked you, they had no choice with me. :) Love ya bro.

To Susan, Whitney, and Kevin. Thank you for being my think tank and sounding board. This book would have taken many more years without each of you.

To South Shore Community Church. Thank you for allowing me to be your pastor. It's a privilege and honor to do ministry with each of you.

To Aubrie and Noah. The two of you motivate me to be a better person and to move past every fear I have ever thought of having. I am so proud of both of you and look forward to seeing you grow into amazing adults. I love you both dearly.

To Lory. Thank you doesn't seem appropriate. You push me to be more than I ever thought I could be. Thank you for your constant support and love. Thank you for believing in me even if I don't believe in me. I can't wait to continue to spend the rest of my life with you. You are the best wife, mother, and ministry partner I could have ever dreamed of. I love you more than words could ever say.

. . . .

CONTENTS

PREFACE

"You must do the thing you think you cannot do."
— ELEANOR ROOSEVELT

"Fear is a manipulative emotion that can trick us into living a boring life."
— DONALD MILLER

This book is meant to serve as a resource and a guide for anyone who is struggling with their fears. We all have them, and how they manifest themselves in our lives is an individual, personal matter. If you're feeling confined or limited in your life due to a crippling, or even an underlying, fear, then I hope you find resolution and a path forward through some of the personal stories and steps I've laid forth in these pages.

But who am I, and how can I help you live a life of intention, untethered by fear? I am a husband to the incredible and supportive Lory, and together we are the parents of two amazing children, Aubrie and Noah. I am a son to Gary and Sandra and a brother to Mike. I am a licensed and ordained minister and a pastor in Sarasota, Florida. I am a friend, a coworker, a musician, an outdoor enthusiast, a part of a community, a student, and a teacher, and above all, I am a work in progress, like many of you.

I've struggled to balance my own fears with my faith, and I've watched others do the same. I've witnessed unspeakable tragedy and been privy to some of life's most precious and beautiful moments too. I certainly don't purport to have all of the answers, but through my experiences, I have learned a few simple strategies for getting unstuck from the debilitating mindset that prevents us from living life to its full potential. Inside this book, I'll share those strategies with you through storytelling.

The fears that gripped me felt so overwhelming and isolating, and I knew there had to be others out there like myself, trying to find a way forward. Part of me wrote this book for that awkward 15-year-old kid I used to be who was not living his life to the fullest. I believe there is a 15-year-old kid inside all of us, trying to figure things out and living in the face of a fear. I wanted to share some of the tools I discovered that helped me find my own way past the fears that isolated me and into the loving and supportive arms of community and friends. My hope is that you will find inspiration in my story and be able to apply some of the things I learned to your own life.

INTRODUCTION

My life changed forever on July 1st, 1987. I was only seven years old. My older brother, mother, and I were at an air show in Fayetteville, North Carolina. My dad was a paratrooper at Fort Bragg, and he was working crowd control at the air show that day. He rarely came with us and usually set out before we did to set up for the show. Our plan was to see him there.

The three of us went to this kind of thing all the time when I was a little boy. My brother and I enjoyed the show as much as anyone, but between the "air tricks" we'd get bored. Usually we kept ourselves entertained by playing army, out of the way of the crowds.

It was a crystal clear day. My mother was sitting high up in the bleachers so she could do two things: watch my brother and me playing beside the dirt runway about 50 feet away and take pictures of the activity in the sky. She was a professional photographer and accustomed to keeping her eyes skillfully trained on her boys and what was going on around them.

A C130 Hercules was coming in for a LAPES maneuver, which stands for Low Altitude Parachute Extraction System. This particular maneuver is used during wartime when the pilot can't land the plane but still needs to get supplies to the troops on the ground. The way it's supposed to work is the C130 swoops down very close to the ground, maybe five to ten feet, and drops a parachute with supplies out of the back.

On that day in 1987, we knew a Sheridan tank was supposed to be launched out of the back of the C130. The pilot was a novice in training. He came in a little too fast and a little too steep, and he realized his error too late to pull back. As he tried to level out, the nose of the plane hit the ground, and he lost control.

Everything unfolded in slow motion. It felt like we were watching a movie, only the scene before us was terrifyingly real. I don't remember every detail of what happened that day, but I very clearly remember being surrounded by several hundred fear-stricken people. The experience of witnessing and feeling fear simultaneously is not something you ever forget.

My mother and brother clearly remember seeing the young pilot furiously try to steer the plane away from the bleachers, which were filled with spectators watching in horror. When the wings hit the ground, the body of the plane was engulfed in flames. The Sheridan tank slid out of the back and skidded down the runway. The fuel from the plane soaked the runway, and the plane headed straight toward some military jeeps, where a few officers had been sitting on to watch the show.

The jeeps burst into flames upon impact. It seemed like the whole world was on fire.

Complete pandemonium ensued. A voice came over the loud-speaker telling everyone to get under the bleachers. My mother couldn't get to my brother and me fast enough through the chaos. She yelled at some random man in the stands to grab us. We were still out by the runway, dangerously close to the flames and the fuel. (The next day, you could see us in the foreground of the crash in a picture that ran in the newspaper. We were that close.) The man got my brother and me to our mother, and the three of us dove under the bleachers for safety with the rest of the spectators. It felt like we were under the bleachers for an eternity as debris and flames rained down all around us. The noise of the fire, the emergency sirens, and people's screams filled the air.

We were terrified, and we had no idea where our dad was. There were about a dozen or so army guys clustered around the burning jeeps, and we thought maybe he was with them. Later, we learned that he had been in that area, but his unit had been moved to a different section of the base to set up for another part of the event that day. Eventually, he found us huddled together underneath the bleachers. Once it was established that we were all okay, he had to go straight back to work to deal with the horrible accident. Finally, we got the go-ahead to clear out and return to our cars.

Later that day, we tried to process the events that had unfolded before us. Through my seven-year-old eyes, it had seemed at first that the flames and the excitement were part of the show. We had seen grand theatrics before, such as parachutes with brightly colored smoke streaks streaming as they glided down through the air and all manner of suspended acrobatics. But this was not the intended drama; we had witnessed a tragedy. Five people died that day, four of whom were on the plane and one of whom was sitting on a jeep and couldn't get out of the way fast enough.

We felt immediate sadness for the people who had been killed and their families, but the impact and the after-effects of the incident continued to evolve for days and years afterward. Every time there's a plane crash on the news—and there have been several this year alone—I feel heartbroken for those who lost their lives and for those who saw the crash, and I am immediately drawn back to that day in 1987.

I'm not sure when exactly I made the decision that I was never going to fly in a plane again, but something in me shifted that day. Despite the fact that my childhood had been full of airplane exposure, I was certain I wouldn't get on one again. My uncle was a recreational pilot, and we had flown with him on numerous occasions. Of course, my father was a paratrooper in the army for 26 years. He retired as a lieutenant colonel in the '90s. As a small boy who had been so close to what would become a life-altering accident, the fear of flying, and of planes in general, had been planted deep within my consciousness.

Throughout my childhood, my family was close-knit. One of the reasons that family is so important is because we moved around a lot due to my father's job in the army. Early on in their marriage, the doctors told my parents that they couldn't have kids. They adopted my brother Mike when he was only 12 days old. Four years later, my mom got pregnant with me. To say that I was a surprise baby would be the understatement of their combined lives. My brother and I have always been very close, and even though he lives in another state now, we remain in frequent touch. No matter where we moved, even though we left friends and loved ones behind, we always had each other, which only strengthened our bonds. Growing up, my brother and I were taught that family is everything.

I was born in Frankfurt, Germany. We stayed there for about 18 months before moving to an area of Cocoa Beach, Florida. From there, we moved to Fort Leavenworth, Kansas. Being an introverted kid and having to start over every two or three years was tough, and we all relied on each other heavily. Once we got to North Carolina, my parents decided my brother, mother, and I would stay put while my father continued to move around the world for work. He lived in Korea for a year and traveled to other exotic ports while the rest of us put down roots.

The church has always played a big role in my life, even as a small child. It was a way for our family to connect with the community, and my parents both have a deep faith in God.

No matter where we moved, my parents always made sure we found a church to go to.

When we got to Fort Bragg, North Carolina, our church pastor, Dr. Drexel Brunson, lived about two blocks away. His son was only a year younger than me, and we became very good friends. I spent a lot of time over at his house, and I got to see a lot of the pastor in his "off hours," as if there is such a thing. What struck me at the time, and I was only about 12 years old, was that man's heart. He was the kind of guy who, whenever anyone called and needed anything, he would drop everything and go. It was through watching him in action and seeing how open his heart was for others that the desire to be a pastor began to foster inside of me. I wanted to be like Dr. Brunson and help people. We moved not long afterward, but I stayed in touch with his family over the years.

Through the church, I went on a number of mission trips around North Carolina, Georgia, and Kentucky, but anytime a mission came up that involved a plane ride, I backed away. If the trip was within driving distance, I was in; if it required air travel, no way.

Only much later in life did I realize one of the effects of the crash was that I became an incredibly safe person. I weighed the dangers behind every choice that crossed my path and behaved accordingly. I'm sure I missed out on doing a number of things that would have been incredible, but those moments passed me by because I always considered risk over reward.

When I was 24 years old, I was presented with the opportunity to travel to Africa for an extended mission trip. My immediate response was "No way." I was already a youth pastor at the time, and though the journey's focus was training other youth workers, I was paralyzed. I had grown so accustomed to simply shaking my head and saying "no," that it had become second nature.

My senior pastor visited me in my office to challenge my response, and he made a strong case. "Listen, Nic. I want you to be a part of this trip. We need you there. I'll help you with funding, and I'll be by your side the whole time." I stayed firm in my resolution, but he pushed a little further. "Maybe you need to pray about this. Instead of just going with your canned answer, it's time to do some searching on what God wants for your life." I thought to myself, "I don't need to pray about this because God already knows how I feel."

I found myself caught in a trap between my fear and my faith. There I was, teaching and preaching to others to put their trust in God, but I wasn't practicing what I preached. When it came to my own decisions and my own fears, I struggled mightily to let go and surrender to God. I was allowing my fear to dictate the strength of my faith as well as all of the decisions I was making in my life. I was at a clear, but certainly not easy, crossroads. I wanted to go to Africa, but my fear told me there was no conceivable way I could get there.

Had I not been a pastor in a traditional Southern Baptist church, I'm not sure that I would have come to this fork in the road at such a young age. In that world, pastors are wrongly put on a pedestal. They're almost not allowed to be human, and they're certainly not supposed to fail or have any problems. Additionally, Southern Baptist pastors put a considerable amount of pressure on themselves to live up to the impression the congregation has of them. I was no different. This scenario created an environment in which I had to face the issue much sooner than I likely would have otherwise.

Through deep prayer and a lot of hard conversations, I was able to slowly peel away the layers of what was holding me back. I learned that you cannot talk someone out of his or her fear or rationalize it away. In response to my fear of flying, people would always say to me, "You're more likely to die in a car crash than a plane crash. Statistics show…blah, blah, blah." Those kinds of comments, as much as people mean well, do not help. None of the "common sense" arguments matter when you're crippled by immobility. I was just trying to figure out how to get on a plane without having a heart attack!

Slowly, reluctantly, I decided to break down the challenge of flying into bite-sized pieces. I had to start small and build up to the 19-hour flight to Africa. I decided to fly to North Carolina from where I was living, which was about an hour-long flight, just to see if I could physically do it. Within that one flight, there were multiple hurdles to overcome, each equally terrifying: stepping foot on the plane, listening to the engines fire up, the preflight speech about crashing, the takeoff, the in-flight time, and the landing. Each step seemed fraught with peril, but I did it.

The flight to North Carolina was the first leg on a long road to coping with my fear of flying. People talk about conquering or overcoming their fears, but I'm not entirely sure that's how it works. I think the experience is wholly unique to the individual, and I can't say categorically that anyone is ever completely "cured" of a fear. It's a lot like addiction. It's something that people will always face, but slowly they are given the tools and strategies so that they learn to live with it. That first flight to North Carolina was like that for me. I discovered that yes, I could physically get on a plane. But that didn't mean that it was easy or that there weren't moments of stress and even some mild panic. However, I discovered I could ride it out.

People tend to get so caught up in the end game without looking at the small victories along the way. If we wait for the grand prize, we'll never celebrate what we've achieved. Dealing with fear requires a marathoner's mindset; it's a long training process filled with barriers. When we can learn to live with our fears, or live in spite of them, we've already made a huge leap forward. I think this slight variation in thinking is an area where many people struggle, but it could be a game changer. They feel they cannot celebrate until the fear is gone. The reality is that the fear may never go away, and that's okay. Dealing with it is a gradual, day-by-day process.

Ultimately, I had to learn how to balance my fear and my faith, instead of allowing my fear to make my decisions. Fear is mentioned in the Bible over 400 times. There are hundreds of examples where God says, "Do not be afraid." There are over 125 direct commands from Jesus, according to Scripture, and 21 of them are related to overcoming fear. Over and over again, Jesus encourages us to fear not, to take heart, and to have courage.

In 2 Timothy 1:7, Paul is talking to Timothy and encouraging him and his ministry. It says this: "For God hath not given us the spirit of fear; but of power, and of love, and of a sound mind." God doesn't want us to fear. In fact, He has given us the opposite directive. He has given us a sound mind and the wisdom to know when to fear and when not to fear. He has given us the love and the power to overcome these moments.

Recall the fears that Moses faced. God called upon him to be a voice for the people. But Moses was afraid because he was a terrible speaker. Scripture says that he had a stutter or a speech impediment. However, he did not allow the fear to stop him. He continued to move forward because it was what God wanted him to do.

Think about the disciples as they rode out and fought a massive storm for nine cold hours in a little boat. What should have taken them 60 minutes took all night, and then the unthinkable happened. They looked up and saw a ghost-like figure walking toward them. Jesus came on the scene and said to them, "Don't be afraid. Take courage I am here!" (Matt. 14:27 NLT).

In that moment, Peter took Jesus seriously. Peter said, "Lord if it is you, command me to come to You on the water." So He said,

"Come." And when Peter had come down out of the boat, he walked on the water to go to Jesus (Matt. 14:28-29). Peter would have never stepped out of the boat or even had the thought to if the waters had been calm. Often times, storms prompt us to take unusual actions.

These types of stories are inspirational, but we already know the outcome. Moses succeeded, and he was a great man. We see the back end, but we don't get much insight into his upfront struggles. Peter knew Jesus, had seen Him do miraculous things, and so he was literally about to step out by faith. Bible story after Bible story follows the same pattern. The truths are easy to see and to accept, unless you happen to be faced with that same struggle in your own life. When you're in the middle of a crisis, it becomes hard to see the tools that God is handing you. We become powerless, but ultimately, we can master our fear. Your fear may not go away completely, but it doesn't have to control you. This book will show you how. I did it, and I know you can too.

CHAPTER 1

NAME YOUR FEAR

"Bravery is a choice, not a feeling."

— JON ACUFF

"Courage is resistance to fear, mastery of fear, not absence of fear."

— MARK TWAIN

"The only thing we have to fear is fear itself."

— FRANKLIN D. ROOSEVELT

There are a few key principles I would like you to consider before diving into this book. First and foremost, fear doesn't make you weird; it makes you normal! People tend to feel so alone in their fears, but everyone has them to varying degrees; most of us just don't wear them on our sleeves for the world to see. Many times, anxiety and worry are the symptoms of fear, and they can become a smoke detector that triggers the real, core issue. If you're experiencing anxiety or worry around a certain problem, or just in general, dig a little deeper to get to the root cause.

I don't know that I would go so far as to call myself "lucky" in terms of my fear, but the tie-in between the plane crash that I witnessed as a child and my fear of flying has always been pretty clear. After I worked hard to break my fear into small bits and was able to travel to Africa at the age of 24, my life opened up. I got to experience overseas travel, see a third world country, and become immersed in a new culture.

However, going to Africa was a nerve-racking endeavor, to put it mildly. Aside from the obvious long plane ride I had to endure, there were several political and cultural factors that made it dangerous for Americans to travel. We were in Zimbabwe, which was facing a time of civil unrest and unspeakable violence. Prior to our departure, we were peppered with literature about how to get out of perilous situations, how to deal with a military confrontation, and the best communication practices with local villagers. We weren't going to jump out of helicopters, but we were told about evacuation protocols in the event of an emergency, which included how to find the U.S. Embassy. Survival went far beyond the 19-hour flight over there and back; it was a daily reality.

I was in Zimbabwe for almost four weeks, but it wasn't until I got home that I began to question myself on a profound level. Why had I been living in such a narrow box? Why did I always play it safe? What is to be gained from that kind of life? My initial response to these questions was because I am a natural introvert, which was a label that had become a crutch. There are plenty of introverted people who are still capable of making big changes and living their lives to the fullest. I clearly wasn't one of them.

Only after some deep and difficult soul searching did I understand that the trauma I had witnessed when I was seven years old wound up making a lot of decisions for me. My path to enjoyment had been hindered. I know that I would have had more excitement and joy in my early years had I been more open to risk, which is not to say that I didn't enjoy a very nice life. My parents were middle class, they took care of our every need, and they were very loving. I simply didn't realize that there was life outside of the bubble I had created for myself. I wasn't even aware that there were things "out there" that I could do or experience that would have changed my perspective.

When I came back from Africa, I was able to see the potential for my life in a new way. A lot of my revised attitude was directly related to better understanding and being able to put a name to my fears. Not only was I afraid of planes because of the crash I had seen as a boy, but I was also afraid of almost any activity that involved risk. Did being able to identify these fears mean that I was cured? Not even close. But it was the first step of many toward learning how to live with those fears and grow through them.

HIDDEN FEARS AND WHAT IFS

I come into contact with a great many people through my congregation, and I am fortunate enough to be viewed as a confidant to several of them. The topic of fear is something that comes up a lot, most often in the context of dying. People fear their own deaths as well as the deaths of their loved ones, which can be a crippling feeling. I've witnessed it first hand on multiple occasions.

Many years ago, I had a good friend who absorbed all of the terrible things she heard on the news and started to fear for her children. She heard about other kids who had been abducted or who had gotten terribly sick, and she thought, inevitably, these fates were lurking around every corner for her own kids. She developed agoraphobia and shut down to the point that she never left the house. She was homebound for almost four years and used every excuse in the book to justify her behavior. She had allowed the "what ifs" to take over her rational thinking. She couldn't leave the house because what if someone got hit by a bus? What if someone contracted a rare and deadly disease? What if someone was exposed to lead paint? Peanut butter? A child molester? And on it went.

It's not uncommon for people to become oversaturated by the woes of the world and internalize them. There are so many things in our society to worry about: job security, the mortgage, your marriage, your career path, and your children. The problem is that we tend to rationalize away our fears or refer to them as something else. We may even try to disguise them with busyness to take the attention away from the fear and change the focus. The fear is still there, but we don't have to think about it.

When we can't name what a fear is, we can't begin the process of balancing that fear with our faith. Often times, people opt for the easy answer. I'm guilty of doing this myself. I played it safe for years and had no idea what I was missing. Making the connection between the plane crash and playing it safe was a difficult correlation for me to see, so I certainly empathize with others who are struggling for clarity. How can you discover what you're missing out on if you can't name your fears?

Sometimes, the best way to get to the root cause of an issue is to enlist others in the discovery process. Ask the people who you are close with to help you. You can even be as straightforward as to say, "Hey, what do you see in my life that is holding me back?" When you allow others in, you benefit from added introspection. Their perspective is not necessarily the gospel, but any insight that helps lead you toward identifying your fear is valuable. Once you can name the fear, it becomes tangible, and you can begin the process of dismantling it.

Fear is rarely found in the safe and comfortable areas of our lives. Those are the areas that we go to hide and remain risk free. So, recognize that fear is what drives you toward your bubble.

Another human character trait is to try to cover up our fears with something less ugly than the truth, largely because we fear ridicule or embarrassment on top of the root fear itself. Fear thrives in secrecy and is fueled by emotions such as shame and guilt. For example, I just pretended I wasn't a very interesting person. I was afraid people would tell me it's dumb to be scared of flying. In fact, some people did tell me that. I hid behind being an introvert. It was an easy excuse for not trying things that were potentially dangerous; however, being extroverted is a large part of my job. I am required to connect with people. It's something that I truly enjoy doing, even though my preference is for one-on-one communication.

A counselor friend and I were talking about the perception of introverts versus extroverts. She explained that being an introvert is less about one's personality type and more about how someone prefers to recharge their batteries. This is definitely true in my case. Whenever I'm tired or emotionally drained, I need to pull away from people and be by myself for a little while. Alternatively, extroverts crave crowds when they need to recharge. Despite the fact that I regularly speak in front of thousands of people, I need to be alone to build myself back up. This is not an excuse for hiding from my fears anymore, but for a long time, it was.

Public speaking is not something that comes naturally for me. To this day, every time I walk on stage to deliver a sermon, I still get a sick feeling in the pit of my stomach. As soon as I start speaking, thankfully, I am able to find my rhythm and the sick feeling dissipates. The fear of public speaking is anchored in another relic from my childhood, which was a speech impediment. I had to go to speech therapy to learn how to enunciate more clearly, and the memory of that time is always in the back of my mind when I have to get on stage.

Just like getting over my fear of flying, learning how to speak clearly in public was a slow and sometimes arduous process. I didn't get up and speak to thousands of people on my first try! I would have died on the spot, undoubtedly. I started with ten or twenty people here and there until I was gradually able to build up to larger numbers of people. Later, I used video recording equipment and got used to being broadcast, and now I speak to thousands of people over the Internet through my church and through my blog. That's what I call progress, if I do say so myself. But I worked hard to get there, and I celebrated each little step along the way.

Close to 80 percent of the population shares the fear of public speaking. It's one of the reasons Toastmasters is such a successful organization. You can find a branch in almost every city across America, and everyone is there for the same reason.

Most fears, however, are not as clear-cut as flying or public speaking. A friend of mine was recently telling me about her grandmother. Today, her grandmother is quite well off financially. However, she grew up during the depression, and the culture of scarcity was a defining aspect in her life. Going hungry and being without basic necessities were realities during her childhood. To this day, my friend's grandmother will not throw away a scrap of food. When her family is finished eating Sunday dinner (or any meal for that matter), she scrapes everyone's leftovers into a big container to make a stew with at another time. Even though she can afford to buy dinner for everyone in the county, she is governed by the fear of running out of food. The ironic part is that she easily spends money in other areas of her life—little luxuries here and there—but when it comes to food, she's practically a hoarder. She's created a system for herself where (in her mind) she'll never run out of food again.

People commonly gravitate toward ritualistic behaviors due to a childhood trauma. Often, what's required is a complete attitude shift. One of my favorite quotes is from a pastor friend of mine in Washington, D.C., Mark Batterson, who says:

"Change of place + change of pace = change of perspective."

In addition to being a pastor, he's also an author and a public speaker. When I first heard him introduce this concept a few years ago, it had a powerful effect on me. When you change your pace, you get out of your routine and slow your life down, which allows you time and perspective. Sometimes you also need to change your place: go on a vacation, get out of your work realm, and open your eyes to different possibilities.

I often reiterate Mark's sentiment to my coworkers because some of them never take a vacation or a break. Changing one's pace and place is essential for a fresh outlook and a new appreciation of things. I honestly believe combining the two leads to a better overall attitude about life. Mark's quote comes back to me sometimes when I'm in the middle of a hectic moment or when everything feels unmanageable. It helps me to slow down and reassess, and it makes things seem less stressful.

STRATEGIES FOR MOVING FORWARD

"The best map in the world doesn't matter if you don't know where you're going."

— JON ACUFF

One of my goals for this book is to show you that no matter what you are facing, no matter how insurmountable it may seem in the moment, there are ways to cope and to get unstuck. Battling a fear is not easy, and it requires time, patience, diligence, self-discipline, and self-awareness. But as someone who has been there, and who still struggles today (I'm human!), I can promise you that it can be done. I've done it, and I've seen countless others do it too. Your life is sacred; you need to put energy into figuring out what is holding you back—and why—before you can fight it.

First, acknowledge there is a problem. If you're reading this, you've already taken the first step! Take the time to focus on the problem. Self-awareness takes practice. People are rarely hit over the head with a light bulb answer. Yes, that's what we are all striving for, but getting there takes time. Until you become self-aware and make a concerted decision to search for that moment, you'll never find it.

In my case, I stumbled into the light bulb quite by accident. Sometimes, it happens that way. All along, I thought I was crippled by a fear of flying (and that was and still is a very real fear), but the reality is, I was afraid of way more than that: I was afraid of life. I was being held back by a self-protective, risk-averse mentality.

One of the best ways to name your fear is to be intentional in your approach. Go buy a journal and write down what you're thinking and feeling. This is a visual exercise because by writing things down, you can begin to unearth patterns and trace events that trigger uncomfortable emotions or responses. Diana Pitaru, a licensed professional counselor with a Master of Science degree, wrote, "The best way to release your fears is to shine a light on them, acknowledge their existence, and figure out their root cause." Make a list of your issues and the people in your life who might be able to assist with each one. This helps to narrow your focus. You may not find the answer immediately, but it will lead you to finding the answer eventually. Take a long hard look at yourself and assess who you are.

Naming your fear is the intentional step of saying, "I need to know what it is, and I need to move forward. When I name a fear, as big or as small as it is, I will write it down. I want to see it everyday so that my mind is focused on that fear. I need to figure this out." It's not something everyone likes to do, but it's a start and it works. The University of Florida Counseling and Wellness Center states, "The first step in handling your fears is to determine exactly what you are afraid of."[†]

"Looking at where you currently are in life turns your present into a platform you can jump from instead of a prison that will hold you back."

— JON ACUFF

. . . .

ACTION STEPS TO NAME YOUR FEAR:

1. Buy a journal.
2. Make a list of your fears.
3. Enlist others to identify/name the problem.
4. Practice self-awareness to better recognize fear-driven behaviors.

[†] http://www.counseling.ufl.edu/cwc/how-to-handle-fears.aspx

HEED THE CALL, BUT DON'T RUSH IT

"Whether you think you can or you think you can't, you're right."
— HENRY FORD

Today, you may not have a fixed plan on how you will tackle your fear, and that's okay. If you have named it and written it down, you are two steps closer to tackling it, and that alone is cause for celebration. When you put your fear in front of yourself and face it, you are heeding the call to cope with it. It means that you've made the decision to deal with it gradually. This doesn't mean that you have a plan mapped out or even that you know where you're going, but you know that someday in the near future you'll address it. You'll break it down into bite-sized pieces and smash that fear to bits.

As Henry Ford said, there is tremendous power behind the way in which you *think*. If you think you *can't*, you've already adopted a defeatist attitude, and you've created a self-fulfilling prophecy. Alternatively, if you believe you *can*, you are open to possibility.

One of the problems with fear is that it can be so prevalent; we decide immediately, "There's no way." I know I'm guilty of that. We don't even allow ourselves the opportunity to make a decision. That is how it was for me after the plane crash. I was resolute and said to myself, "There is no way I am getting on a plane ever again in my life." I wasn't even going to try. I became my own canned response. There was no thought process in it, and because I already knew the answer (no way), of course, I was right.

BABY STEPS

We've touched on my trip to Africa that kick-started the necessity to overcome my fear of flying. I'll share with you some more details about how it came to pass because that trip was pivotal in my journey of facing my fear head on. I hope that by sharing this story, you will be inspired to try something new too, no matter how hard it may seem today.

Several people from my church had already been on the Africa mission trip, including my senior pastor. I'd heard the stories about how incredible and life changing it was, even for those who weren't terrified of getting there. One part of the trip was to train and educate other pastors on how to grow their church and reach more people. Of course, the economic and religious systems in Africa are worlds apart from the way they are here, so there were clear challenges up front that required out-of-the-box thinking. Essentially, this trip would be a three week-long brainstorming session to find out what was working in their community and what wasn't. Then together, we would devise strategies for increased outreach.

The second portion of the trip consisted of a vacation of sorts to see the country. The plan was to go to a wildlife preserve, sleep in a tree house, and engage in other activities specific to the area. I knew all of this promised to be fulfilling and rewarding in unimaginable ways, but prior to being approached about going, these kinds of opportunities weren't even on my radar. There was a part of me that wanted to see more of God's creation than I was able to see within a drive, but I rationalized that I could fulfill that desire while still playing it safe.

The senior pastor and I had a special relationship. He was a mentor to me, and we were friends. We used to play ping-pong together whenever either of us needed a break from studying. He would come into my office and silently lay a paddle on my desk, which meant it was time for a game. It was during one of these infamous ping-pong matches that he challenged me to make the trip and advised me to pray about it. I told him flat out, "I don't need to pray. God knows perfectly well why I don't want to go, so there's nothing to say or pray about on the matter." He pressed harder and said, "Nic, I know this will change your life and later your entire view. Give the matter some thought." So, reluctantly, I did.

I prayed, and I spoke to close friends and relatives. After some counsel, a lot of counsel, I decided that I should at least try. I booked a flight to Raleigh from Atlanta, where I was living at the time. The flight time was about one hour. My thought process was, "I'll get on this plane and see if I die." I was running through all of the "what ifs" that I could possibly imagine. This flight was after 9/11, so the what ifs ran along these lines: What if I have a panic attack? What if the plane is hijacked by terrorists? What if the plane blows up in midair? What if we crash?

But the wheels were in motion, and I had slowly started to switch over to a "maybe I can do this" mentality. It was a tiny, but also enormous, step forward. I know that's a contradiction, but that's how it was. My mindset was changing. The first step was realizing that *maybe* I could, and the second step was booking the ticket. I was scared the whole time, but I could feel what was happening. It felt good.

The initial exercise of flying to Raleigh was something that I had to conquer alone. I had let my fear control me for so long, and my battle with it was so personal, that I didn't want to drag anyone else along for the experience. I needed to prove to myself that I could do it, and I didn't want anyone else to see me freak out or have a panic attack. All of those thoughts were running through my mind, so by the time I got myself to the Atlanta airport, to simply park my car, I felt like I had climbed the Himalayas.

Actually getting on the plane came with a whole new crop of challenges. I'll never forget the sick feeling I had when the engine revved up for takeoff. The stewardess played the video of all the things that can go wrong during the flight and what to do in the event of an emergency. As if all of those things weren't already on a steady loop in my mind! (Apparently a small seat cushion was going to save my life.) I was clutching the armrests with my eyes squeezed shut, and I was praying furiously the whole time, "God, don't let this be it. Please don't let this be the end of me." Thankfully, once we were airborne, it was a pretty smooth trip and free of turbulence. I may have loosened my grip slightly on the armrest and peeked out the window for a second or two. As you can imagine, I experienced another moment of terror when it was time for the landing, and I was white knuckled the whole way down. We landed safely, and I had never been more relieved in my life.

Odd as it may sound, it never crossed my mind that I would have to get home when and if I survived the flight to Raleigh. I had spent so much time and energy preparing to get there that I completely overlooked the necessity of a second flight, which is a testament to where my head was at the time. I kind of assumed I would talk myself out of flying back and instead rent a car to get home. The minute I landed is when the reality of getting back home occurred to me. The truth is that I didn't believe that I actually would survive the first flight. Nowhere in my mind did I think I would succeed. I had a classic defeatist attitude.

Fear and hope do not get to occupy the same space in our hearts. We have to decide which of those emotions is going to stay. Most of the time, fear wins because fear fights harder than hope. When you allow yourself to celebrate the small victories, you are helping hope to win the fight in your heart. The flight to Raleigh was all about allowing hope to bloom in my heart, and on that day, it blossomed. I was still terrified of flying, but I knew that I could do it. I had two more tickets to book: first stop, Atlanta—next stop, Africa.

When I got home after my initial plane trip, I was excited—but nervous as all get out—to tell the senior pastor I was ready to tackle the Africa mission trip. He knew as well as anyone what a big deal this was for me, and he was thrilled at the turn of events. I was still primarily focused on the 19-hour flight to get there, as opposed to the actual mission work itself, but that's what fear will do to you—take over your brain.

Because of the length of the journey, my "what ifs" took on a new dimension: What if the pilot gets tired and we crash? What if we run out of fuel mid air? What if I have a panic attack half way through the flight? The fears began to stack one on top of another. Luckily, there were video games and movies and other in-flight distractions to take my mind off of things. Plus, on a flight that long, most people sleep for at least half of it. I welcomed the down time and the opportunity to be occupied by something other than the fear loop.

There were parts of the flight, though, that were truly horrible and very bumpy. We landed on a small island west of Africa to refuel, and I was not excited that we had to take off and land again. Next, we landed in South Africa on a patch of dirt that can hardly be called a runway. From there, we needed to take another plane to Zimbabwe, which happened to be the oldest, most run-down hunk of junk I had ever seen in my life. Even the seasoned travelers among us were scared to board that thing.

After almost a full day of one harrowing experience after another, we finally arrived at our destination. My nerves were fried, and I was utterly exhausted from the stress. It was exciting that I had overcome so many obstacles in a single day, but I needed to recuperate from all of the emotional energy expended.

Once we rested, we met with the missionaries who were to serve as our guides for the trip. I leaned on them heavily while we were in Zimbabwe, not only for every day advice and help but also for spiritual support. The political unrest and violence led to several scary situations, in which case I trusted our guides to navigate the system and get us out safely. Even when my faith wavered, I could rely on theirs to see us through. Their faith was already strong and tested. They knew the area, they knew the rules and dangers, and they had overcome them. There was a perception that because they were living in this land, they would be okay. Even in those moments when my faith caused me doubt, I knew I could look to them. I found tremendous comfort in being able to count on others in a situation such as that, and I am eternally grateful to them for their hospitality and knowledge of the area.

There were countless cultural differences that we had to learn quickly. It was almost like going to the doctor when he tells you everything that could possibly go wrong or even listening to the stewardess during her preflight terror spiel. We were told, "Don't wave. You could get shot. Do give a thumbs up as a friendly gesture. Don't drink the water. Don't eat the food. Don't get bitten by a mosquito." We got all of the appropriate shots and vaccinations in advance, but Zimbabwe is a country with an abundance of foreign issues and diseases.

I was reminded once again of Peter's predicament in Matthew 14. He asked Jesus if it was Him who commanded him to get out of the boat. It was, and Peter did the unthinkable. He defied gravity, science, and nature and began to walk on water. After a moment, he took his eyes off Jesus and began to see the dangers around him—the storm and the waves—and he began to sink. When he began to sink, Jesus reached out His hand, caught him, and said, "You of little faith, why did you doubt?" (Matt. 14:31).

This story stayed with me throughout my time in Africa. I knew Jesus had called me to go, but that didn't mean that my trust stayed fully on Him every step of the way. Like Peter, there were days that I faltered and looked at the situation I found myself in rather than Jesus.

All in all, the trip was life altering in so many ways. We would be riding along in an open-air jeep, and out of nowhere, a herd of elephants would pop up. They came right up to the car. Our driver always carried a gun in case things became dangerous. He would nicely explain that they could flip a jeep in an instant. We were on a boat one time, and hippos came swimming up right beside us. The guide explained that they could destroy the boat in no time. You can see the constant reassurance I was lacking.

Aside from the incredible animals, the people I met were wonderful. It was eye-opening to meet people who were so much less fortunate than I was growing up, but who still had unwavering faith and were genuinely happy. Many of them had faith and joy stronger than I had ever seen in anyone. Everywhere I turned in that country, I saw, felt, heard, and tasted something new. I truly got to experience the awe of God's creation and marvel at the world all around me.

There were heartbreaking moments too. We were visiting a village, and one of the missionaries instructed us not to share our snacks with any of the children who approached us in the market. I thought it was the cruelest policy because these kids could have been starving. Later, he explained that if you give something to one kid, before you know it, there would be hundreds of kids in the shadows waiting, swarming you. They would get mad if you didn't have enough for everyone, and the situation could quickly turn into an angry mob. I had never considered the danger of simply carrying a snack in my backpack before. My instinct is to give things to people who ask or who are in need. There were so many subtleties to adjust to.

We visited Zimbabwe in 2004, which was at the absolute pinnacle of the political unrest. The country had a string of vicious dictators who killed anyone who didn't agree with them. They seized huge parcels of land, and everyone was afraid for their lives. Seeing the very real fear in the eyes of the people I encountered was a humbling experience, and yet, their faith was strong. They lived with so little in the way of comfort, yet possessed a joy I had rarely seen. They loved God and trusted Him despite the reality of their daily lives. I was not comparing their lives to their neighbors; I was comparing it to my own. If I lived in the same types of conditions, I wasn't sure that I would have been able to be as happy as they appeared. It made me realize that often the source of our joy or happiness comes from the wrong place. We shouldn't be looking for joy in our circumstances or in the things we surround ourselves with. We should find it in God.

When I returned home from Africa, I started to think a lot

about my own fears and the impact they had on my life. Up until that experience, I would have never considered myself to be a person with regret, but I started to understand how much I had been missing out on. It was a feeling similar to driving down the highway with a dirty windshield. The glass is so obscured that you can't even see what you're driving past. In this analogy, the dirt is our fears. It clouds our vision and prevents us from having a complete experience. Some of the things we're missing could be dangerous or bad, yes, but most of it is not. The fear is blinding us to everything, and it's overwhelming. We don't have the right tools or the strength to overcome it. By breaking the fear into small pieces, it becomes more manageable and doable.

"Do you not know that in a race all the runners run, but only one gets the prize? Run in such a way as to get the prize."
— I CORINTHIANS 9:24

If you were training for a marathon, would you lace up your sneakers and go run 26.2 miles on the first day? Of course not! You'd be hospitalized. It's far more effective (and healthy) to devise a sane and safe training program. Most people who are in training have tremendous self-discipline. If they fall off the plan one day, they're up and at it again the next day. You must approach tackling a fear in a similar manner. It's a step-by-step process, which begins with naming it and then laying out tangible steps to begin to move past it.

For me, it was simple, which is not the same thing as easy. I needed to know that I could survive on a plane. The flight to Raleigh was a big step comprised of several other smaller steps.

One step forward leads to the next step, and the next step, and so on. Maybe the first mile you run feels impossible, but tomorrow, once you've done it, you'll run two. In a few weeks time, the idea of running 26.2 miles will become a distinct possibility (just like flying to Africa!).

ACTION STEPS TO HEED THE CALL:

1. Break the fear into manageable pieces.
2. Lay out tangible and measurable steps.
3. Celebrate small victories.
4. Lean on others for support.

CHAPTER 3

FEAR AND FAITH

"Where we put our attention, we put our intention."

— UNKNOWN

A BALANCING ACT

For as long as I can remember, the church has been a huge part of my life. My faith in God is something that has always been with me, but its strength has varied at different times. Growing up, and even as recently as a few weeks ago, I've always heard that if you are fearful, you don't have enough faith. I have a hard time accepting that statement, and frankly, I don't agree with it.

Matthew 17:20 says, "Truly I tell you, if you have faith as small as a mustard seed, you can say to this mountain, 'Move from here to there,' and it will move. Nothing will be impossible for you." This is the type of faith the Bible teaches. It is not about the "amount" of faith you have. The tiniest amount of faith can move a mountain. So if it is not about how big your faith is, why is your faith not pushing you past your fear? I've given my life to God, but I still have fears. Just because I have faith doesn't mean my fear has vanished. There is a balance between the two, and I believe the issue comes down to which are you fueling—fear or faith. Best-selling author and preacher Max Lucado once said, "Feed your fears, and your faith will starve. Feed your faith, and your fears will."

The matter comes down to a decision. Where are you putting your energy? A similar corollary can be drawn to personal health and nutrition. I'm a health coach in my free time, and one of the mantras for healthy living is, "What you put in is what you get out." If you eat clean and are intentional about what you put in your body, you will achieve the outcome you are looking for. If you choose healthy foods, invariably you are moving toward a healthier lifestyle. It makes logical sense that if you eat junk, you will feel like junk. Just because I know this doesn't mean that I always live it. It's hard.

Where are you focusing your attention, and is it in harmony with the direction you want to be heading in your life? This is an important question to ask as it relates to balancing fear and faith. Let's banish the misconception that being fearful equals a lack of trust in God. The two are not mutually exclusive.

Faith can be a struggle for people at certain times in their lives. It's also harder than simply telling someone to just trust in God and to forget all about any fear. When we direct people to think and behave in this manner, we are setting them up for failure. It's almost impossible to ignore a problem or a fear. If the person is not able to simply put it aside and trust, they will inevitably feel even worse about themselves, which only compounds the problem or fear. Now he or she is also worrying about being a failure in God's eyes. We have to allow people to deal with life's realities while still trusting God.

Think about the disciples in the Bible. They witnessed Jesus perform some pretty unbelievable feats: healing the blind and the sick, turning water into wine, and walking on water. You would think that the disciples would never doubt or question their faith because they had seen these miracles first hand. But time and time again, when pressed, they would waver. Jesus didn't belittle them; He simply continued to teach them and show them the power of God. He was patient and forgiving and nonjudgmental. Yet often, when our faith wavers, we beat ourselves up, or maybe it is other Christians who do. Faith isn't a now or never choice; it's continually growing in the face of challenges and doubts.

The same can be said for almost any endeavor that one commits to in life—whether it's your career, your fitness regime, or your marriage. We are all constantly trying to improve, to increase our knowledge and awareness. The more you do something, the better at it you will become, whether if your efforts are intentional or not. Faith is the same way. It's something that needs to be practiced and improved upon constantly throughout life.

As children, our faith is unwavering. My kids have faith in everything. They have faith that when they jump off the monkey bars, I'll be there to catch them. Over time, as they become more independent, their faith will start to dwindle. Slowly, they will need to learn how to build their faith back up. We're all the same way. We need to work on it steadily over time. Through faith, we can experience tremendous freedom and peace.

Fear, on the other hand, is something that creeps up on us and takes us off guard. We feel overwhelmed and powerless by it. It holds us back and ties us down. It's very hard to have faith in a fear moment because often, those moments can be paralyzing. Of course, there are healthy fears as well, such as fear of your elders, fear of God (which is out of respect and awe), or fear as it relates to anything that might impact your safety. Ironically, it's within the paralyzing fear moments that our faith begins to grow and build.

Unfortunately, as a child and a young adult, I constantly felt like I wasn't living up to the expectations of the church. I thought I was failing at every turn because my fears were holding me back. For example, whenever an opportunity came up to go on a trip involving air travel, I had to say no because of the plane crash. There were moments when I said to myself, "Man, I can't do this. Obviously, I don't have enough faith in God to get over this fear, but everyone else around me seems to have enough. I must be doing something wrong."

My self-esteem took a beating due to my constant internal battle. There is nothing worse than being immersed in a Christian community and doubting your faith. That's not supposed to happen! But the reality is the dual dynamic happens to everyone all the time.

For years, I struggled with the fear that I wasn't a good enough Christian because I had fear. Can you see the cyclical nature of that scenario? Fears compound, and they thrive off insecurity and doubt. I was worried that I didn't trust God enough in certain areas of my life. I felt like if I didn't hand everything over to God, including all of my fears, then I didn't love Him enough. I know many others have struggled with this same issue. Even the most devout and religious people I know have endured periods of wavering faith.

These moments still happen to me today, even after years of studying and learning. We're all human; we're not perfect spiritual specimens. Instead of letting the self-doubt and feelings of failure hold you back, slow down in the moment and say to yourself, "Okay, why is this happening? Where is my faith lacking, and how can I fix it? What am I missing, and how can I go about doing better?" I try to remain very conscious and not get into a cycle of beating myself up. I know that doing so is counterproductive, exhausting, and a waste of time.

One of my main goals for writing this book is to help people feel free in their relationship with God. I know I felt very un-free in my religion for a long time, and I don't want others to suffer through the doubt. The church has a tendency to be very rule centered, so much so that people feel restricted or guilty if they can't hand everything over. I believe that God's heart and the Bible's message is one of celebration and freedom, and I want to spread that love and remove any ill will.

As a pastor, I'm proud and happy to say that the people I talk to tell me they feel free. They have come alive in the recognition that their relationship with God does not need to be hard. You don't need to feel guilty, bad about yourself, or afraid. Church can be very freeing in this regard if you find the right community and open your heart to God. The church doesn't set out to alienate people from God, but unfortunately, so many times that is exactly what winds up happening.

STRATEGIES FOR RECONCILIATION

There are two ways to embark on the mission of balancing fear with faith: first privately through introspection and self-discovery and second through community. When you look at your fears and faith individually, hopefully, you're writing things down and visualizing a plan for moving forward. When you enlist the help of others, you are gathering the troops to help with the attack.

Community is one of the biggest enemies of fear. "Strength in numbers," as they say. Fear likes to keep you isolated and trick you into thinking that you're in this all alone; no one understands what you're going through, and if you tell anyone, they will either laugh at you or tell you you're stupid. When you can find like-minded people who have gone through what you're going through, they become your safety net.

"If you listen longer, you'll go further faster."
— ANDY STANLEY

Stanley is essentially saying that your best path forward is to gather the advice of others who have been there before. Ask them what they did to get through it and allow others to see your vulnerabilities. No man or woman is an island, although fear would have you think otherwise. It's much easier to shift your focus away from whatever is eating you up inside when you're surrounded by other people.

As a pastor, I need to write a sermon every week. There are times when I simply cannot think clearly anymore. Maybe I've lost the direction, or I can't find the right analogy to demonstrate my point. When those moments occur, I get up and go look for a distraction. It does me no good to sit quietly and stare at the computer, waiting for inspiration. I need to get up and go find it and move my mind into a different area. Even when you are not focused on the immediate problem in front of you, your mind is still working on it. You're just not actively engaged in the process.

The same strategy works with fear. Through distractions, our minds become clearer. We become less focused on the anxiety or worry, and we're able to free up some space to experience laughter or joy. Before you know it, you can return to the problem, or the fear, and see the answer that you may have been searching hours, days, or even months to find. The one small step of getting up and finding something else to do allows you to see what you couldn't see before. Maybe the distraction is just taking a walk, playing a few holes of golf, or having coffee with a friend. Maybe it's a game of ping-pong with a trusted advisor. It can be anything in your life that brings you relief and a chance to let your mind engage in another activity.

Much of the advice that I share in these pages is related to a philosophical shift in your mindset. It's not about overcoming; it's about learning to live with your fear or issue. It's about building better patterns and better habits for coping.

I was at an AA (Alcoholics Anonymous) graduation meeting recently to support the graduates and celebrate their achievements. While there, I was thinking about how the 12 steps don't end with the graduation certificate. Those 12 steps continue throughout the rest of an addicts' life. Even after graduation, they're told if they hit 90 meetings in 90 days, the likelihood of their continued success will skyrocket. The AA program is not just about accountability; it's about creating healthier habits.

I believe the fear/faith balance conundrum comes down to a similar mentality as the AA program. We have to know that when we continue to take small steps forward, eventually we will achieve a measure of success. And when we're not strong enough to weather the storm alone, we need to lean on other's faith to see us through.

"Lean on me when you're not strong, and I'll be your friend. I'll help you carry on."

— BILL WITHERS

When I was in Africa, I needed to lean on the faith and knowledge of my missionary guides, and they saw me through. The reason I was able to trust in them was because they had already been through what I was facing; they knew my own fears intimately, and they had already successfully survived the experience. They were where I wanted to eventually be from a faith perspective, and because of them, I got there.

It's important to find people to lean on who don't have exactly the same fear that you are experiencing. Think about this. If you're afraid of heights, do you really want to attempt climbing a mountain with three other people who are also afraid of heights? No way. You'll all be struggling the whole time. You want to find someone who has already climbed that mountain. In doing so, your anxiety will decrease dramatically because you'll be with someone you can trust who knows the ropes. It's the exact same scenario as when you're traveling abroad. You find a guide to show you the way.

My guides in Africa were a husband and wife team who had lived there for several years by the time I arrived. They also knew all of the pastors we would be interacting with on the trip. Our guides spent every day with us, drove us from village to village, and made sure that we had everything we needed. They basically oversaw our entire cultural immersion. There was definitely a language barrier, but most of the people we encountered under the age of 25 spoke English or some variation of broken English, and they were excited to practice their language skills on us. We required a translator for anyone older than 25, and I had an interpreter for any preaching that I did while I was over there. I had practiced a few words and key phrases ahead of time, but I relied heavily on others to translate.

The overarching goal of our mission trip was to train church leaders. Because I was a youth pastor at the time, I was specifically focused on helping church leaders better connect with the young people in their communities. As a group, we also led some outreach programs. We were taken to a few deeply impoverished areas to better understand what the church leaders were up against. For example, locals were accustomed to the power going out for days at a time or the petrol stations being without gas. As Westerners, we can barely fathom such inconveniences for more than a few hours at a time, but in Africa, it was an almost daily occurrence. However, the people we were with remained unbelievably positive and joyful in spite of the setbacks they faced.

We were lucky to be warmly and well received by our guests and the locals. I clearly remember one man who walked for two days to come see us. Think about that. There were no hotels to stop at for the night or convenience stores to grab food and drinks. He simply walked and slept on the side of the road. He had lost both of his hands as punishment for a petty crime he committed when he was much younger. He heard we were coming to share the Gospel and made the trek from his village. He didn't speak any English. We needed a translator to communicate with him, but his hunger to hear about God and to meet us was palpable.

We were similarly received by most of the people we met. They were all starving for somebody to give them something, and they had a lot of questions. The pastors we were working with faced challenges we had little to no experience dealing with, such as tribal rifts and other barriers from ingrained traditions. They also had to contend with a lack of resources or land with which to build a church or gathering place. They found creative ways of overcoming most of the immediate obstacles they faced, and I was in awe of their continued ingenuity.

Even when we feel we are alone or without answers, God is there in the other people around you, giving you an olive branch or a helping hand. You have to start looking for God's influence in people and situations where you may not expect to see Him.

He places people in our lives who will help show us the way. These are providential encounters or relationships that help to properly frame a situation. The importance of community cannot be underestimated, so pay attention to who is standing right in front of you.

My senior pastor and ping-pong opponent is one of the few people on earth who could have challenged me on my fear about flying to Africa at that time of my life. He was standing right there when I was ready to cross my bridge of fear, and he gave me the friendly push I so badly needed. My pastor was the providential relationship for me in that moment. I likely would not have responded in a similar fashion if the push had come from another source—but because I respected this man and knew he had my back, I felt like I should try.

No one should go through the highs and/or lows of life alone. This statement is a core belief of mine. I believe in building an intentional community; one that will be there through the exciting, celebratory times (a new baby, a job promotion, over-coming a fear) as well as the dark times. My wife and I are both self-proclaimed introverts. We could easily stay at home all day with each other and be quite happy, but we also know that we need to foster relationships with those around us. It's an active choice and one that is necessary for our mutual and individual survival.

When you have community, you have people by your side to walk through your fears. Those specific people have been chosen by God and placed in front of you for a reason. He isn't going to force a relationship, but He will give you the tools you need to build your own network. He's given you free will and the mindset and the skills to get out there and do certain things with your life.

"Direction, not intention, determines destination."
— ANDY STANLEY

We can want to get over our fears, but if we don't set out on a path to do so, we'll never get there. We need to have some clear sense of where we are going and what the path will be. Intention alone is not enough.

* *

ACTION STEPS TO RECONCILE FEAR AND FAITH:

1. Awareness: Where are you focusing your attention? Is it in alignment with the direction you want to be heading?
2. Remember: Faith must be practiced. It cannot be taken for granted.
3. Gather your community. There is strength in numbers.

CHAPTER 4

LOVE AND ADVENTURE AWAIT

"Death is more universal than life. Everyone dies but not everyone lives."

— ALLAN SACHS

FIND YOUR CALLING

My day-to-day life is given meaning through the wonderful people whom I get to interact and work with. In a strange way, these work relationships are similar to the partnership I enjoy with my wife in that my coworkers and staff support and challenge me to be better every single day.

I find joy in being able to reach others. When I was initially called to become a preacher, it was never because of the actual "preaching" side of it, being on a podium and speaking publicly in front of large groups of people. I was drawn to helping people and being a part of their lives, the way I saw Dr. Brunson from Fort Bragg to be.

Back in high school, I was part of a youth group, and I remember that I never really fit in. I was terribly awkward, chubby, and reserved. I wanted to focus on youth pastoring in my early years because I wanted to create a safe and welcoming environment for misfit kids like myself. I wanted to make a difference in their lives because those kids always need a little extra help feeling noticed. These days, I oversee the program and am not directly involved, but as a team, we strive to make sure no one falls through the cracks and always feels that they belong.

I love to see teenagers find the gifts that God has given them. When they can stand in their own skin and celebrate their unique attributes, the light that shines within them is truly inspiring. I tell people all the time that I have the greatest job in the world because I get to watch young people come to life in Christ and see how their lives are changed as a result. I get to see them find their own joy and their own gifts and their own freedom. It's an exciting thing to be a part of. Admittedly, most of the time, I feel like I'm sitting in a movie theater watching it all play out. They are doing the work themselves, and I just get to watch! Even though conquering a fear may mean triumph over something very small, the implications are tremendous. If you're only focused on the "big" win, you'll have far less opportunity to celebrate, and every single small victory is cause for celebration.

People ask me all the time what it's like to be "called," and every minister will have his or her own story. For me personally, it was an overarching feeling of knowing that being in ministry made me happy, and whenever I was away from it, I was unhappy. I'll give you an example. A good friend of mine is a baseball player, and I feel like he was called to play. It's his overriding passion, and he loves it more than anything. He got a bad injury playing and had to sit out on the sidelines for about a year. I can tell you that it was the most miserable year of his life. He was still making money, but he wasn't able to do what he was called to do.

Being called is the feeling of knowing that you can't do anything else because **this** (ministry, baseball, teaching, writing, parenting, fill in the blank) is what you are meant to be doing. It's not about the money or the glory; it's about the feeling that you're at your best when you're at it. It makes your heart sing with joy. This is exactly what it's like to be called to ministry.

I come into contact with a lot of people every day who are not doing what they have been called to do. Maybe they are making a ton of money, but they are unfulfilled. Maybe they are in a career just to make ends meet, but the day-to-day doesn't come close to reaching their hearts, let alone making it sing. I adamantly believe that everyone on this earth was put here for a specific purpose, and if you're not living in it, you're probably not that happy. I always try to tell people to find what they love doing and do it! Maybe you cannot build a whole career around it, but you can make it a part of your daily life in some way.

A huge part of doing what you love comes down to realizing that contentment has to come from what God has designed you to do, not from what you make. I'm fortunate that I realized this early on in life. Money doesn't fill the holes in your heart; only joy can do that. I'm no billionaire by any stretch, but I make a decent living, my family is taken care of, and I am doing what I was meant to be doing. Therein lies the joy!

The most rewarding aspect of being a pastor for me personally is helping people to find their calling and live a life they love. When someone is able to realize what they were chosen to do, they also realize that God loves them unconditionally. I am often with people in their darkest hours, but having the privilege of walking beside them during their highest moments more than makes up for the sadness and tragedy we often bear witness to.

This characteristic of caring was what I saw in Dr. Brunson and what I loved about him. He was with people when the light was shining down on them, and he was there in the darkest of nights. I remember my parents used to tell me stories about him. Even when the phone rang at 3:00 a.m., he did his best to sound perfectly awake. He didn't want people to feel they were inconveniencing him with their phone call. That's what I call living with intention! He thought of even the smallest details and put himself fully in the presence of the people he was helping.

MIND SHIFT

A part of me has always wanted to see the world. I spent so many years silencing that side of myself and letting the fear do the talking. Once I made it to Africa, the amazing cultures and sights of the world were overwhelming but intoxicating. I thought to myself, "Wouldn't it be incredible to experience new things all the time?"

I view the trip to Africa as the moment my life began to open up, and I started to look for the other things that I had been missing out on. My eyes had been opened, and the shift in my soul was seismic. When I got home and started to settle back into the routine of daily life, my mind wandered to all of the places I still wanted to visit. I started to research different locations and learn about their histories.

My perspective started to change as I explored new possibilities. I spent more time daydreaming about the future and taking things into consideration that I had previously deemed impossibleeveryday, little things. I actually started a list, which grew in length to the point that I thought about turning it into a book eventually.

Prior to the trip to Africa, I had been living what I considered to be "The American Dream." I had been striving for things that didn't really matter in the grand scheme of things: a cool car, a big house, and a bigger salary. After spending time with people from another culture, I realized that joy isn't found in the things you don't have; it's found in an appreciation for the things you do have. I feel a little ashamed to admit, especially as a pastor, that it took a journey outside of my comfort zone, to the other side of the world, to truly grasp the concept.

I'm sure I had been preaching about appreciation prior to the trip, but teaching something and living it are two completely different things. The Africa trip solidified the idea that true joy lies within our own hearts, not in obtaining more things. Even though I wasn't making a ton of money as a youth pastor, I was pretty wrapped up in materialism. I just hadn't realized how much.

Today, I live for the relationships in my life. I treasure the deep connections I have with God, my wife and kids, my coworkers, and my congregation. My wife is an incredible woman who takes care of our two children and me in the most loving and supportive way imaginable. Our children are still very young, four and five, but we are proud that they are respectful and well behaved. We believe that children don't need to be crazy and wild at all times; there are outlets for craziness and fun, and we encourage them to let loose when it's appropriate. We encourage them to behave by showing them that we love them all the time and by setting clear boundaries. Being a parent and sharing in that responsibility with my wife is one of life's overwhelming joys.

Lory and I met, strange as it may sound, online in 2005. Online dating was not nearly as widely accepted back then as it is today, and it was something I was nervous about trying. The options for meeting people to date as a pastor are pretty slim. If you date someone from your church and things don't work out, it can be a disaster. The person might leave the church, and then (trust me) things get weird quickly. Lory and I connected over the phone. She was living in Florida, and I was in Georgia at the time. We talked for several months before we met in person, and during that time, we built a solid friendship long before we ever actually sat down to dinner together. We didn't want to tell anyone we met online at first, but now it's just a part of our story that we laugh about.

When we first connected, I was going through a bit of a strange time with my church in Georgia. Working in churches isn't at all what most people assume it is. There are actually a lot of politics, which can be a huge distraction from why you may have sought the church out in the first place. It's not all glam and glory. I can assure you of that. As a young pastor, I was drawn to the ministry because I wanted to serve Jesus, and I just assumed that everyone else did too. You would guess that everyone would get along. However, people are people, whether they're in church or not, and I grew disillusioned by what I found at my church in Georgia.

I took about a year off to do some hard thinking as to whether I had the chops to love people who didn't necessarily love you back and try to help people who perhaps didn't want to be helped. I knew I loved God, but I wasn't sure that I loved all of the people of God. The whole year, I struggled being away from ministry. I had a great job in another field, but my heart wasn't in it. The further away from ministry I was, the stronger the calling was to return.

Ultimately, the internal career struggle led to a deepening of my faith. I realized that I did want to be in ministry, unequivocally. I had a gift that God had given me. Lory and I were in frequent communication during that time and knew we wanted to be together, so I started to look for a church in Florida. The one that I found was in Tampa, about an hour away from where she lived and worked as dental hygienist.

Making the move from Georgia to Tampa was fraught with fears. As an introverted person, moving to a new area is never a fun activity. I experienced that nervousness several times as a child, and I wasn't terribly excited about the prospect of facing all of that newness again as an adult. The job I had accepted was a part-time, interim position, which wasn't exactly stable or long-term. I thought to myself, "Man, if this job doesn't work out, I've uprooted myself from my home base. I'm chasing a dream and trying to live closer to someone I'm falling in love with, but if that doesn't work out either, what's it all been for?"

Before I left for Tampa, I talked to a lot of people who had made similar, potentially life-changing moves. I had friends and knew people in the ministry who had taken similar leaps of faith, so I made sure I had a solid support system in place. I was getting better at this game of tackling fears as I matured. Lory and I saw each other on weekends and whenever we could, until we decided that we should get married. Once we did get married, she moved to Tampa, and our lives took on another, entirely new dimension.

EXTREME HONEYMOONING AND BEYOND

As anyone who has planned a wedding is aware, it's so easy to get caught up in the millions of details that go into the event. We were no different than anyone else and quickly became swept away in the specifics. We talked a lot about the honeymoon and decided we wanted to go somewhere extreme; somewhere neither of us had ever been, and somewhere we would probably never go at any other time in our lives.

We chose Tahiti and Bora Bora. We saved up the money and planned the trip of a lifetime. But of course, my old fears crept in. It was 16 hours of flight time to get there, and my new wife would have to sit next to me and see my panic attack first hand.

I was almost as worried about her seeing me in such a mess as I was about the flight. We had to travel through California and spend the night, so the journey to get there was extended even longer. Unsurprisingly, we made it there just fine, and the experience was well worth the anxiety before hand.

Lory and I went all out on our honeymoon. We wanted to celebrate that our lives were changing with each other in a big way. We stayed in an open bungalow with a glass floor suspended above the water, which was beyond extravagant. At night, the fish and the other marine life swam up to the lights under our bungalow and gave us our own private underwater show. It was a magical sight.

Then we were reminded just how powerless we are in the face of nature. The outer bands of a cyclone were going to make a direct hit on the island. We knew about it ahead of time, but we didn't have a full understanding of how close it was. The Internet there is very slow, and there wasn't much information about it online. That night, the waves were splashing in through the bottom door of our bungalow, and we were pretty scared. Before the storm hit, the hotel offered us another room on land, but by the time we decided we wanted to take it and move to safety, the room was no longer available. The hotel staff said, "Sorry, you're just going to have to ride it out in the bungalow."

Luckily, we were fine! Some of our activities were impacted the next day, but it was nothing too devastating. We were supposed to meet up with somebody named "Shark Boy" who was going to take us swimming with, you guessed it, the sharks. He cancelled because he was concerned about how choppy the water still was after the storm. Lory and I discussed this and decided that swimming with the sharks wasn't something we could reschedule, so we found another guide who was willing to take us out and off we went. Everyone talked about that activity as one of the best things that you can do in Bora Bora, and we weren't about to miss out just because "Shark Boy" got cold feet. Yes, I saw the irony in this change of heart of mine! First Africa and then Lory had opened my eyes, heart, and mind to new and sometimes crazy possibilities.

When we swam with the sharks, we were in the company of paid professional guides. For that reason, I trusted them. Although I was scared out of my mind, we had done a lot of research about the activity and knew it would be an unforgettable experience. It absolutely was; we still talk about it and look at the pictures to this day.

Our honeymoon to Bora Bora was three years after my trip to Africa. It was a fantastic reminder that there is a whole world out there to see. While we were on our honeymoon, Lory and I got to share a lot of "firsts" together, including a jungle safari tour, snorkeling with sharks and manta rays, and even old school scuba diving where we were hooked up to the air on the boat. As a newly married couple, we explored so many incredible sights above and below the sea. It inspired us to make a list together of all the places near and far and all of the things big and small that we want to try together. We've already been to New York City, Las Vegas, Breckenridge, and Hawaii. We put a good portion of our resources toward these trips because traveling to new places together fuels our relationship and our curiosity about the world.

Each new adventure brings with it a new challenge to overcome or something exciting from the bucket list. We went zip lining over and through the jungle in Hawaii and hiked up a volcano, both of which are contrary to my personality. At the same time though, I've noticed that once you get a taste for something, you start to long for it. Travel and adventure have elicited that effect on me; after all that anxiety from my past, I now crave new experiences.

One of the activities that I had presumed was on my "No Way" list was scuba diving. Although, it was about five years after the trip to Africa and a few years after Bora Bora that I actually learned my brain was churning on it for a while. I'm fortunate to live near the water, but the ease of learning a new sport still took some time to get my head around.

I'm not going to lie; I was terrified by the idea of strapping an oxygen tank onto my back and diving into the ocean. This was a different kind of fear than the fear of flying had been. Although if I hadn't learned to cope with the flying portion, I would have never attempted to tackle the sea. I didn't have traumatic childhood experiences related to the water or to drowning; scuba diving just seemed, on the whole, like a very unsafe endeavor. My father was an avid scuba diver for as long as I can remember, but that didn't do much in the way of ensuring the safety of the activity. Let's not forget this was the same guy who jumped out of airplanes during his 26 years in the army!

Scuba diving was something on my bucket list, and I encouraged Lory to do it with me. At first she had no desire to try it and had a lot of fear around it. Even on the day of the first class, she said, "I'm sorry, but you're just going to have to go on your own." Well, she wound up coming at the last minute, and now she absolutely loves it! There are times now when she and I will get in the water fearlessly, and it's the best feeling on earth. We still have a healthy fear of and respect for the ocean and its powers, but it's a good fear because it keeps us aware.

THE SKY'S THE LIMIT

Dealing with your fears is just the beginning of living the life that you've always wanted to live and are meant to live. Fear holds us back from more than we even know. It doesn't just add the stress of tomorrow but takes with it the strength of today. Fear's goal is to make us shut down completely.

"What no eye has seen or what no ear has heard, and what no human mind has conceived..."
— I CORINTHIANS 2:9

This phrase from Corinthians is referring to the things God has prepared for those who love Him, which is cited in the last part of the verse. There is a whole world of things out there that we have not seen or heard because we are held back by our fears. In Scripture, King David is an example. He was a shepherd and was told that a giant named Goliath was tormenting the people in his village. He knew he had to take on the giant to protect God's people, but he was afraid. Up to that point, he wasn't a warrior. He was simply a shepherd. He had fought off some animals that tried to attack his sheep, but that was the extent of his battle experience. He decided to let his faith outweigh his fear, and with every small step that he took toward his encounter with Goliath, the stronger he became. Ultimately, David was ready for the big battle, and the rest is history.

* *

ACTION STEPS TO FIND LOVE AND ADVENTURE:

1. Do what you love.
2. Be open to possibilities.
3. Leap and the net will appear.
4. Make a list of adventures your fear is keeping you from experiencing.

FEARING FOR SOMEONE ELSE

"The semi-truck of parenting comes loaded with fears."

— MAX LUCADO

When you're young and single, there are likely not very many people in your life who depend on you. Later in life, if we get married and raise a family, it stands to reason that there are added pressures and fears due to sheer numbers. It's not at all uncommon to be concerned about immediate members of your family.

I think everyone can relate to being worried about an elderly parent or grandparent. As we get older, we become more and more a generation of caretakers. I know several people who are caring for their aging parents as well as their own small children, and these compounded responsibilities come with additional stresses and concerns. Some of them are financial, which is normal; most people want to provide a comfortable lifestyle for their families.

As parents, there is a strong tendency to be overprotective of your children. Modern psychologists have dubbed this hovering style "helicopter" parenting to describe those parents who don't let their kids out of their sight for two seconds.

My family lives in a condominium development, which is very safe, and we often see children playing unattended outside. Whenever I see that, I look at Lory and shake my head. There's no way I am ready to let my kids do that. Am I being overprotective, overbearing, and acting like a helicopter? Am I preventing my kids from living their lives or making their own mistakes, even if it means they might get hurt? The more times have changed, the more fear gets placed on our kids.

PARENTAL FEARS

One of my biggest parenting fears is that I will inadvertently transfer my own fears onto my children. I don't want them to be disproportionately afraid of things. Just because I happen to be afraid of heights and avoid roller coasters at all costs does not mean I want them to feel the same way. On the contrary, I want my kids to have all of life's thrills and experiences from their own, unblemished perspectives.

In John Maxwell's *21 Irrefutable Laws of Leadership*, his first law is "The Law of the Lid." I interpret "The Lid" to be the lid that we put on other people when we attempt to control their behaviors. Maxwell is talking about leadership, but I utilize his law at home with my kids. If I tell them they cannot do something, I am immediately putting a lid on them in that particular area of their lives. Is that a fair thing to do? No, not entirely. Throughout their lives, people will put lids on them; as a parent, I don't want to be one more person restricting their potential. We all have lids on us already that other people have put in place: parents, teachers, or employers. We put lids on ourselves too when we tell ourselves we can't do something. To be healthy and to grow in life, we all need to learn how to loosen our lids and let in a little air!

Unscrewing your lid is a big part of being self-aware. If you don't know your lid's on too tight, how can you do anything about it? Take a good look at yourself and your life and ascertain where you are limiting yourself and then ask why. Through the process of looking below the lid and understanding what's there, you are taking the steps to find enhanced freedom.

I need to constantly remember to look at my fears and be careful not to pass them on to my kids. This means also paying close attention to what they respond to. Perhaps my daughter approached the slide without any fear yesterday, but today she seems nervous about it. What's changed? Is the slide wet, or are there other bigger kids roughhousing around near the steps? Did she come down a little too fast yesterday and freak herself out? What's going on, and where did her fear creep in? What has changed in her mindset?

We also need to be aware of when we might be playing it *too* safe. Of course, being too safe is different for everybody. When you are close with the people in your community and notice someone pulling away, it's okay to say, "Joe, has something happened? It's not like you to steer clear of the annual Christmas party." Or, "Mary, I saw you avoid interacting with Marcie last Sunday. Is there anything I can do?" Let others know that you see them and that you are there for them if they appear to be dealing with something differently. You never know what kind of response you'll get, but put yourself out there for someone else. Being a part of a community means that you walk side by side with your people and help them break free of whatever is holding them back.

As parents, or simply members of the community, we've all borne witness to some undesirable behaviors, from adults and children. How you address the issue comes down to the question, "Do you have the right to intervene in this person's life?" If you see a grown-up behaving in a manner that is holding a child back, the first step is to build a relationship so that you can then gain access and earn the right to speak up. You'll never find the right footing with that person if you lead by attacking their behavior or offering uninvited parenting advice. First of all, the person will likely not listen to you, and secondly, you may have closed the door by crossing a boundary too soon. There is a fine line between intervening and respecting someone's privacy or personal choices. Obviously, if someone's life is in danger, there is no choice but to intervene.

A parent's fear around their child will vary depending on the child's age. Since my kids are still very young, I worry if they are liked at school, if they are being picked on, and if they are adjusting to the classroom. As they get older and become more established socially, my fears will shift to more age appropriate concerns. I don't even want to think about when they're teenagers! Each stage of life is different and requires a new balancing act.

FUTURE FEARS

Future fears are the worst because they are the "what ifs" of life. We all have them, and how closely we listen to them dictates how free we are to make our own choices. We've looked at the "what if" scenarios before in terms of my fear of flying, but when it comes to parenting, those ugly "what ifs" can look like many things: How am I going to provide for my children throughout their lives? What if things don't work out with my job? Are these kids going to need their own cars to get to all of their activities? How are they ever going to be confident, self-sufficient adults? Will they find someone to love them? Clearly, these fears are ridiculous, especially for someone like myself with children so young. Nevertheless, we set the patterns for their lives now, at a very early age.

"Start children off on the way they should go and then even when they are older, they will not turn from it."
— PROVERBS 22:6

From day one, parents create boundaries and set their children's morals as guidelines for living. At my house, Lory and I are helping our kids to become who God created them to be, and we are giving them a foundation for the challenges that lie ahead. I'm sure a lot of other parents are trying to do the same.

I look to my children's individual interests to find their strengths.

I am intentional about not allowing them to give in or shut down in the face of their weaknesses, and I try to help them grow in the areas that they are naturally gifted. My son, who is four, is a natural athlete. Don't ask me where that comes from because neither my wife nor I are athletically inclined in the slightest. My son can easily beat his older sister in a running race, and he seems to have more energy than anyone I've ever known. We encourage him to run around and be active; he loves it, it wears him out, and it's good for his growing body!

My daughter, on the other hand, is an artist. She is meticulous in her creativity and pours a great deal of thought into each and every picture. I was called into her class one day to speak with her teacher and was told, "Nic, you need to talk to Aubrie. She is taking twice as long as anyone else to do her art projects. This is a real problem." I said, "Sure, of course. Can I see some of her drawings?" Then the teacher pointed to Aubrie's artwork on the wall among her classmates. I took one look and said, "I'm not talking to her about this. If my kid's making something that looks that good and it takes her a little bit longer, I'm proud of her. She obviously finds joy in it, she's good at it, and she's engaged." Why on earth would the teacher want me to tell her, "Everyone else is doing the artwork faster than you. Hurry up."? No way! Lory was laughing at me when I got home. I don't mean to be a difficult parent, but come on! That teacher was trying to put a lid on my kid.

TRANSFERRED FEARS

I'm someone who is very self-aware, especially in regard to my fears. It's one of the reasons I decided to write this book;

I want to help others learn to be self-aware about their fears and learn to cope with them. Nevertheless, it's easy to see the worst of yourself mirrored back at you through your children. They pick up on everything!

For example, I don't curse, but when things are really bothering me, I'll say, "dang it." I've heard both of my kids say, "dang it" and use the phrase at exactly the correct moment to express frustration. Oh no! My bad habits are rubbing off on my kids. I'm sure all of the parents out there have had a similar experience, perhaps with a more offensive phrase, but it's hard not to crack up in the moment. They obviously learned this phrase from me, but there are a few they've borrowed from my wife too. The kids are helping, unintentionally, to make us even more self-aware! They mimic behaviors you may not have even been aware of.

A common concern among parents is they don't want their kids to have the same problems that they had. Every generation is trying to improve their lot for the next round, and we certainly don't want our kids to face the same struggles we've faced. We have the ability to make the decision to change, and it often starts with ourselves first. This is where modeling the appropriate behavior comes into play instead of behaving how you might otherwise. It can be a daily challenge.

My son has a habit of ignoring direct questions. He's not doing it to be disrespectful; he is just in his own world sometimes and focused on other things. I've gotten into the bad habit of asking "right?" behind every statement. So, sometimes a statement like this comes out of my mouth. "That was awesome, right?" Unsurprisingly, now my son does this as well. He frames all of his statements with "right?" It drives me doubly crazy because I implemented it to curb a behavior and now he mimics it. Now we both need Lory to point out when we are doing it, and don't worry, she does!

Community plays a huge role in molding the mind and behaviors of children too. Parents are far from the only influences on their kids, and sometimes voices from outside the home can be invaluable. One of our son's teachers mentioned to us that Noah was struggling to pronounce a word. We hadn't really noticed, or assumed it was just his age, but once we started to pay attention, we noticed it all the time. We were so grateful that someone pointed this struggle out to us so that we could concentrate on it at home. This is a an example of a little daily occurrence, but as far as my son's speech pattern and pronunciation is concerned, it made a huge difference. Maybe I was oversensitive to Noah's issue because of my own speech impediment as a child. Regardless, I don't want him to have to suffer the way I suffered, and I'm grateful to the person who pointed out the problem to us.

Not all parents are as intentional in their approach as Lory and I are. I do not sit in judgment of those other parents; rather, I understand well the challenges that we all face as individuals and how those issues ricochet throughout one's life and relationships. I am friends with one family in particular who will not allow their teenaged children to participate in overnight church activities. One can argue that it is healthy for both the children and the parents to experience time away from one another. Specifically, I have invited the teenagers on several overnight youth trips through the church, but every time, they decline. I know that these kids would develop some strong bonds with the other children their age and enjoy the experience of having a little independence. I'm not close enough with the parents to intervene or share my opinion, and I certainly haven't been invited to do so.

With everything, there must be balance. I understand that it can be scary to put your children's safety into the hands of another person. These parents are not comfortable even letting their kids stay out after dark. At what point does this level of restriction become unhealthy for the children's growth? Sometimes we lean so hard on our own fears that we are actually causing others to suffer or to miss out on life's opportunities. Parents do this all the time without even being aware of it.

On the other end of the spectrum is a friend of mine who has two kids in college. Her motto has always been, "Don't bail. Let them fail." She knew that if she was constantly hovering over her children, in classic helicopter parenting style, they would never learn for themselves. There are certain moments when stepping in is appropriate, but most times, kids will be stronger adults and have more confidence when they're able to figure things out on their own. We end up trading the need for safety with the loss of adventure, which can lead to a pretty dull existence. There should be a healthy dose of each.

"In all of us, there's a desire for comfort, security, and no risk. We all have that desire, but the moment we get those things, another part of us complains that our life has no real significance because we trade one for the other."
— CHRISTINE CAINE

My son was learning how to ride a bicycle recently. I put the training wheels on, and we went into the neighborhood to practice. He was so excited to learn how to ride and to cruise around with his sister. I have to admit that I'd never put training wheels on a bike before, and I obviously put them on too high. We weren't out there for a few minutes before my son fell and scraped his knee. His wipe out was due entirely to me, and I felt horrible, especially because afterward he didn't want to go near the bike again. He was done. All of that initial excitement was gone and now he was terrified (and crying).

My job as a parent, and as the person responsible for his initial failed attempt on the bike, was to walk him through his fear of falling again. Patiently, I explained the problem with the training wheels to him, we made the necessary adjustments together, and slowly and reluctantly, he climbed back onto the bike again. I held onto the back of the bike, and we started out going very slowly to allow him to get comfortable again. Eventually, he was ready to let it rip. This experience mirrored the similar one we had on the playground a few years earlier with the monkey bars. I'm all about the baby steps. When it comes to the top rung or flying through the neighborhood, I get a little nervous. But the last thing I want to do is stir up any residual fear in my son, especially when he just overcame it! I have learned to bite my tongue, and as my friend says, "Don't bail. Let them fail."

YOUR KIDS' FEARS

When I took my kids to the playground for the first time, they had a small dose of fear about climbing the jungle gym. They had no desire to get to the top rung, and I wasn't about to tell them they had to get to the top. My job was just to show them they could keep going higher, one small step at a time. In the moment, I changed their focus so that they were distracted by me, instead of how high they had climbed. I was there to catch them if they fell.

The same is true in our relationship with God. We need to remember that He is there to walk with us. He is there to catch us if things don't go as we planned. If we are focused on the obstacle or the fear, we miss the opportunity to focus on God. Just as with my kids, I try to redirect their focus to something that brings them comfort in moments of distress. At the end of the day, they usually do make it to the top of the jungle gym. Even though they want to get down right away, their pride is still evident when they run and say to their mother, "Mom, did you see me? I was at the top!" They immediately begin to celebrate the very thing they thought was too big for them.

Invariably, the next time we go to the playground they will want to scramble right up to the top of the jungle gym again. I'd prefer for them to take it a step at a time, as opposed to flying all the way up to the top. Then the dance begins; I'm trying to push them forward while keeping my own fears out of it.

It's hard to predict how a single incident will affect individuals differently. My mother, brother, and I and hundreds of others witnessed that tragic plane crash at the army base in North Carolina. Why was I the only one in my immediate family scarred by the event? My brother didn't develop the same fear of flying and penchant for safety that had hampered me from living my life to the fullest. What can that be attributed to?

Everybody deals with things differently. How we respond can be related to age, what our other fears are, our past, our present, or just how we cope. There are so many dynamics that go into one's residual reaction. My brother's fears are completely different than mine, and he's always been an adventurous person. To this day, he rides his Harley and lives life the way he wants to. The point being that you just never know what will trigger a potentially lifelong fear.

DISNEY WORLD

Of my children, my son Noah is the safer and shyer of the two. It takes him a while to warm up to people. My daughter Aubrie is much more social than her brother and loves to meet new people. One of her favorite things to do is to go to Disney World and have breakfast with the characters, who she considers to be "her friends." She loves to walk into that room and see all of her favorite Disney stars. My son, on the other hand, hates it. He usually screams his head off the whole time. It's a tough experience because my daughter is in heaven but at the expense of my son, who is miserable. I know that if he was able to move past his fear of these characters, he would love the Disney breakfast as much as his sister, but until that day, it's just been something we have to cope with.

Well, the annual Disney breakfast took place about a month ago. Lory and I were hoping that since Noah was a little older this time, his fear would have dissipated somewhat. He had been excited about the breakfast all morning, but when we got into the room, he started to shut down. I know his personality pretty well, and I could see that he was uncomfortable. I was sitting next to him and explaining who the characters were and trying to keep him calm. Out of the corner of his eye, he spotted Goofy and began to freak out. I said, "Listen, Buddy. If you calm down, I'll hold your hand the whole time that Goofy is over at our table." He nodded bravely, we held hands, and he began to calm down. In fact, he remained calm for the rest of the morning.

Noah and I held hands during Goofy and Mickey's table visit, and after that, he relaxed into the rest of the character visits. He realized that the Disney characters were not there to hurt him, and he began to have fun and enjoy the experience. At the end of the breakfast, we were walking out, and Noah grabbed my hand again. He said, "That was fun, Daddy, right?" (There we go with the "right?" issue I mentioned earlier!) I said, "Yes, that was a ton a fun, Noah." He admitted, "I was still a little nervous and scared, but that's okay." My young son had just embodied the struggle and balance between fear and faith. He divulged that he was afraid and then acknowledged that the reward was worth the uncomfortable feeling. Even today, a few months after the Disney breakfast, whenever Noah sees photos of that day, he reiterates his fear in the moment, but says it was worth it. Together, we sat with his fear and quietly rode through it.

* *

ACTION STEPS TO OVERCOME FEARING FOR OTHERS:

1. Ask: Where are you limiting yourself (or others)?
2. Ask: Do you have the right to intervene in this person's life?
3. Build relationships to earn the right to speak up.
4. Don't bail. Let them fail.

CHAPTER 6

YOU NEVER FULLY OVERCOME

"True faith manifests itself through our actions."

— FRANCIS CHAN

Faith is a lot like a muscle. It needs exercise. The problem is we want faith in Christ to be a magic pill or a winning lottery ticket that simply fixes all that ails us. No one likes it when their faith is stretched or pushed much like their muscles, but the results are rewarding.

The Bowflex machine in my bedroom reminds me every day of how much I despise the process of getting and staying fit. In fact, right now, it is an efficient receptacle for clothing. I know though that when I dust it off and actually use the machine and start to sweat, I am getting closer to my fitness goals. I've encountered a lot of people who view their faith in a similar manner.

Having an accountability partner is an effective approach to practicing and training either the mind or the body. In exercise, my wife is my partner. She pushes me when I am unmotivated or would otherwise blow off a workout. We all need people in our lives to help us get up and get going. As a friend, a parent, or a member of your community, it's your job to also help push people through their fears and their faith.

THE NEVER-ENDING JOURNEY

A hard truth that I've had to learn to accept is that we never fully overcome our fears. We hear the terminology all the time in everyday conversation. Words such as "conquer," "abolish," and "banish" populate our terminology, and I feel it leads to a misconception around fear. We look for the big moment when the fear is gone and we are free from its shackles. I think this expectation can lead to some pretty devastating consequences and disappointment because we are never entirely free from our fears.

Even though I have flown in planes several times since my initial flight to Raleigh when I was 24, I still experience fear every single time I fly. I keep waiting for it to go away and never return, but I don't believe that day will ever come. I am significantly less afraid than I was before, and I am able to board a plane without an embarrassing, public anxiety attack. However, the minute the plane hits a rough patch in the sky, I return immediately to my terrified seven-year-old self and imagine the plane crashing to the ground in a sea of flames. The fear is still alive inside of me.

When we talk about "overcoming fear," we need to change the expectation that we'll be "cured." We need to shift the focus from the big picture to the small frame where we take the baby steps to slowly be able to *live with our fears*. When you get on a plane, climb on the bike, tackle the Bowflex, scale the monkey bars, or invite your community into your heart, you're taking small steps toward the end goal, and every single one of those small steps should be noticed and celebrated. Maybe you're not going to fly around the world, ride in the Tour de France, or climb Mt. Everest, but you are learning to cope with what was once a paralyzing fear.

The big moment, truth be told, rarely comes. Once I realized that truth, dealing with my fears became so much more obtainable, and by default, easier. When you break the mountain down into a series of hills, you stop looking for the peak, and it's such a tremendous relief. The trick is to learn how to manage your fears so that you can live with them, instead of being imprisoned by them.

A perfect example of this is Jesus Himself. In Mark 14, we find Jesus in the Garden of Gethsemane. The writer describes Jesus in verse 33 as being deeply distressed and troubled. Matthew agrees as he describes Jesus as sorrowful and troubled (Matt. 26:37). This is a side of Jesus that we hadn't really seen yet. Throughout all the miracles that Jesus performed and the situations Jesus and the disciples found themselves in, He was always the one pointing out the solutions. Yet, in this story, we find Jesus struggling with fear of the worst-case scenario: He would face the wrath of God.

He went into the garden to pray and brought some of His disciples with Him. He told them to wait and pray, and He did the same. His prayers were that God would take this cup from Him. He prayed over and over again. He asked His disciples to pray for strength. Jesus wasn't imprisoned by His fear. Instead, He gathered His community and went to the one source that could either stop His fear from coming true or guide Him through it. Hebrews 5:7 says, "During the days of Jesus' life on earth, he offered up prayers and petitions with fervent cries and tears to the one who could save Him from death." Jesus lived with His fears by handing them off to God.

WHEN BAD THINGS HAPPEN

There are times, unfortunately, when our worst fears do come true. The world is filled with unspeakable violence and tragedy every day, and there are times when the worst of the worst lands on our own doorstep. I'm thinking of the big Ds: death, divorce, disease, and disaster. There are things that we have absolutely no control over. In times such as these, our natural human response is to withdraw. In no way am I going to tell people how to react to personal tragedy that has impacted their lives, but when you're ready, ask for help, seek out those you love, and start the process of rebuilding. I've learned that there is a time and a place for preaching and a time and place to just be quiet and listen.

As a pastor, I talk to people dealing with unimaginable tragedy every day. My job is strange in that I am with members of my congregation on the very best and worst days of their lives. I get to participate in the weddings and children being born, but I am also called in when someone is dying or is given terrible news. I'm on such a crazy journey with my own highs and lows, and to be given the opportunity to participate in others' major life experiences as well is a gift I am honored to be given. When you're close with people, you celebrate and feel all of life's hurts with them, side by side. Nobody should ever tell you it's time to move on. The decision to step out of darkness is a deeply individual and personal one.

In the face of smaller issues, or what I'll refer to as setbacks, is when the real danger kicks in. The tendency is to simply stop chasing our dreams or attempting to overcome the obstacles that pop up. In those cases, having a friend push you in the right direction can be just the ticket, especially if you're in a place where you can't see the road ahead clearly yourself.

Practicing self-awareness in day-to-day moments when the smaller setbacks happen is an invaluable tool. I have had to stop myself in the moment several times and reexamine the situation, and it helps tremendously to gain clarity. When Noah fell off his bike when I was trying to teach him how to ride it, my heart just sank. I could have said, "Okay, that's it. We're going inside. This was a failure." But for some reason, I was able to recognize how important the moment was in my son's life and how my reaction would be remembered. I had to push through my own disappointment and feelings of remorse to get my son back up on the bike. We needed to slow down, regroup, and accept the fact that something bad happened and that we could move forward anyway. These are the steps necessary to prevent an accident from turning into one of life's paralyzing moments.

Last year, Lory and I went to New York City for the first time. We were so excited to explore and be exposed to the all of the experiences of a big city. We were heading out for a day of sightseeing, and I suddenly realized I forgot something in the room. I told Lory to wait for me in the lobby while I ran back up to the room, which was on the 43rd floor. I got into the elevator and all of the lights were off. I didn't notice right away because the light from the lobby was pouring in. As the doors began to close, the darkness took over and my mind began to race. I have the same healthy fear of elevators that most people have, and I started to worry that I was going to be stuck. At the grocery store in Florida, they just rolled out a new energy-saving tactic with the store lighting. I hoped the NYC hotel was trying something similar, but the lights never came on. I was fiddling around with the buttons and hit number 43 and the doors closed. The elevator started moving, but I was in complete darkness.

At that point, I started to panic. I was praying that the elevator would just stop, and I could jump off at whatever floor it stopped on. I wasn't thinking clearly, otherwise I would have simply hit a lower numbered floor button. The elevator continued to climb as I imagined every terrible scenario possible until eventually it stopped on the 43rd floor, the doors slowly opened, and the light from the hallway poured in. I realized I was safe and that I would be okay. I have never been so thankful to get off of an elevator in my life. It was one of the scariest moments of my life, but taking the stairs to the 43rd floor was not an option. I had to keep riding in strange elevators for the rest of the trip. The experience was just one of those times when I had to find a way to move forward, even though I was terrified.

Looking back, I can clearly see the warning signs. I have thought of several different ways I should have handled the situation as opposed to just riding it out in a cold sweat. At the time, I was in such a state that I didn't even notify the front desk there was something wrong with the elevator. Only later, after a few days passed, did it cross my mind that I should have told someone. Fear numbs you to common sense and being proactive.

SELF-PROTECTION

Have you given any thought to what your limitations are? Knowing what you can handle and knowing when to put the brakes on in terms of stress is a critical component to balancing life's highs and lows. I talk to new pastors about the importance of finding a middle ground all the time, especially when it comes to helping others with the extremes that life deals out. It's necessary to set up some guardrails, which means knowing when enough is enough and knowing just how much you can handle. Honestly, how helpful can you really be to someone else if your own nerves are frazzled?

There are days when I need to regroup internally after work before I interact with my wife or kids. I don't ever want to put on a fake face with them, but I also don't want for them to see me worn down. On those kinds of days, sometimes I'll just sit in the car for an extra few minutes to collect myself. Occasionally, I need to lie down on my bed for a little while and clear my head.

Part of being a pastor (or a friend, a spouse, a parent, or a teacher) means that when the people in your life go through something, you go through it with them. This can take an enormous toll. There was a boy in one of my first youth groups who lost his father to leukemia. He was about 15 years old, and I was 24. We weren't that far apart in age, and we were good friends. My heart broke as I watched him grieve for his father. As a young pastor, I was supposed to be there for him and comfort him. I learned quickly that being there doesn't mean being fake. It means if he's hurt, I hurt too. His pain was my pain, and I realized that there is nothing to say in those moments of profound despair.

A few weeks after his father died, my friend sent me a beautiful letter. He thanked me for all of the wonderful things I said while he was going through the worst experience of his life. I know I didn't say anything! I sat in silence with him and grieved. It's not about what you say; it's about being there. I still have that letter all these years later because it had such a deep impact on me personally and on my career as a pastor. That letter is a good reminder to me that being present in someone's life is more important than anything else.

When you're walking through a period of struggle, surround yourself with your support system. You don't have to fill them in on every single detail of what you're going through, but you should let them know that you are facing a tough time. The more open you are with people, the more they can help. Bringing others into the fray is part of identifying your fear or issue and embarking on a process to deal with it.

Some people are naturally inclined toward solitude. Perhaps they don't have many friends or close family they can depend on, or maybe they don't want to be a "burden" to others. (I hear that statement from a lot of people.) Still, there are others who are truly going through a period of isolation and simply don't have a community available. I empathize with the latter scenario because I've been there.

There was a time in my life when I moved to a new town, I didn't really know anyone, and I was living in a one bedroom apartment alone. It was likely the darkest time of my life. I had a job working in a bank, but I wasn't friendly with any of the other employees. I went to work, stuck mostly to myself, and then went home to my empty, quiet apartment. Because I felt so alone, I wasn't taking the time to invest in the people who did come into my life. I promise you that everyone has someone they can lean on. Maybe you're not very close with the other person, but it's better to spend time with someone you don't know very well, or even someone who drives you a little nuts, than to be completely alone.

Seek out community. Church is a phenomenal place to find other people to connect with. There are several thousand people that attend church in Sarasota. We've created smaller groups within the larger population of the church as a way for people to more easily connect with others. A church our size can be overwhelming. We recognized that and try to make our community accessible and approachable for newcomers. We have a wonderful, full-time staff to help people find the right group that matches their interests.

Every week, I receive emails from people who have just moved to town and are looking to meet new people. They usually share a little bit about themselves, and I am able to determine where they might connect well. If you're living in a lonely space, it can be a struggle to get outside of yourself. Once you are able to do that, connecting with others becomes so much easier.

When I was living in that dark period of solitude, I had to force myself to seek others out. It's a really hard thing to do, especially if you're an introvert. Eventually, I did find a group of people that I could open up to and share some of what I was going through. My connections were so devoted that I found I had almost zero down time; my new group of friends always wanted to hang out. One of my new friends would just show up at my apartment and say, "Let's go do something fun!" The people in your life are what propel you forward through the rough patches, so scratch the surface and find a group of like-minded individuals to share your life with. You'll be happily surprised to learn how eager others are to help and support a newcomer.

GET A GAME PLAN

If you are dealing with a fear or facing an issue that feels insurmountable, the best course of action is to get a game plan in place. Remember, you may never fully overcome it, but we can learn to live with our fears. Set some milestones for yourself instead of sitting around and waiting for change to happen. When you have a fixed goal that you've written down, you can more easily hold yourself accountable. Say to yourself, "Two weeks from now, I will have talked to both Ruth and Ronald about XYZ." Write their names down, and once you've had the conversation, record their feedback. This exercise is imperative for goal setting. The goal, of course, is to build a community. You're inviting others on your journey, and from there, you can set the next milestone.

What are the next three or fours steps you need to accomplish that will bring you closer to your goal? Write it all down and map it out. If one of the steps feels too big to bite off, break it down into even smaller steps. Although it may seem as if your game plan will take months or years to achieve, you must be proactive in your approach. The longer you sit with fear, the larger it grows in your mind and the less likely you are to take action. The more you stare at a problem, the bigger it seems and the more powerless you feel.

Taking measurable steps demonstrates that you are planning to succeed. The same approach can be applied to almost anything that you are trying to accomplish in your life: weight loss, career success, relationships, and the list goes on. I've struggled with my weight for my whole life, and I've found that what works is to break my goals down into small, attainable action steps. Instead of focusing on the piece of the puzzle that feels insurmountable (losing 50 pounds), I look at the micro-picture (I'm having grilled chicken for lunch). Analyze what specifically is holding you back or preventing you from approaching your struggle with an attitude of success. If you don't know exactly what is holding you back, ask others to help you identify the issue.

"Do not be anxious about anything, but in every situation by prayer and petition, with thanksgiving, present your request to

God, and the peace of God, which transcends all understanding,
will guard your heart and your minds in Christ Jesus."

— PHILIPPIANS 4:6-7

In handing things over through prayer and thanksgiving, God will grant us a measure of peace and strength. That peace will help us to move forward, and we can know that God is with us, by our side. We are not on the journey alone.

. . . .

ACTION STEPS TO ACCEPTANCE:

1. Find an accountability partner.
2. Know your limitations.
3. Seek community.
4. Have a game plan of small steps and write it down.

CHAPTER 7

LIVING IN THE LIGHT

"Fear may fill our world, but it doesn't have to fill our hearts."

— MAX LUCADO

Every day is an opportunity for a fresh start. Don't miss out on all of the incredible gifts in your life by choosing to stay in the darkness. We make the choice. Where will you put your attention, and what will you choose to focus on?

When Lory and I went to New York City for the first time, we were drawn in by all of the attractions. The brochures showcased the highlights, the incredible skyscrapers, the lights of Broadway, the high-end shops, and the amazing food. But when we arrived, what I saw was garbage. It was piled up everywhere in stacks taller than me. Street after street was littered with mountains of trash. I was completely blown away. Maybe there was an extra surplus of trash because we were there right after Thanksgiving, but my immediate thought was, "This place is dirty." I couldn't understand it. New York is one of the biggest and best cities in the world. Why would the people who lived there tolerate such filth? You'd think they would have the resources to handle the garbage in a better way.

Later on that day, we checked into our hotel and got dressed to head out for a night on the town. We walked around Times Square and were drawn in by the lights and glamour of everything. Our eyes were drawn upward to the gigantic glittering billboards and flashing advertisements. The trash was still there all around us, but we didn't notice it anymore. We were focused on other things and lit up by all of the excitement around us.

How one copes with fear is similar to how I reacted to the garbage in New York City. It all comes down to what you're focusing on. If you are looking at the good things in your life, you can move forward in small steps past the fear. Sure, there's trash all around the streets of New York City, but there are also other beautiful, mind-blowing attractions and architectural feats at every turn. The streets of New York that night were the same ones we had walked along during the day, but we just saw them in an entirely different way.

WHEN YOU'RE TESTED

The journey from darkness into light can be arduous; there is no doubt about it. The speed with which you get there depends on how intentional you are in your approach as well as what you choose to learn from the experience. I'll share a personal challenge that affected my family, how we responded to it, and how it changed our perspective.

As you know by now, I come from a tight-knit family. Through the years and the miles, we've remained very close, and we rely on each other for emotional support. Our closeness is not something that I've ever taken for granted. On the contrary, I've known many people whose families are divided, and I've seen the toll that strained relationships take on the family members. I've always cherished the relationship I have with my parents and brother, and I know it is unique.

A couple of years ago, my father had a heart attack. I was living in Florida, and he was up in Georgia. He had been feeling bad and mentioned as much to some friends, who thank goodness, encouraged him to go to the hospital. It was there he learned that he had a heart attack the day before. I got the call that he was in the hospital on a Thursday but was told he was okay. Nevertheless, I was still extremely concerned even though we spoke on the phone and he said they were taking good care of him.

On Saturday, my mom called and told me that my dad had been rushed into surgery. She said things were not looking good, and I needed to get up there as fast as I could. Lory and I were in Tampa on a business trip. There was no time to go home and pack. She just dropped me off at the closest airport, and I got on the next flight to Atlanta. When I finally got to the hospital, my dad was in a coma, where he would remain for close to a month.

The doctors had inserted a balloon into his heart to keep it pumping. The balloon was just a temporary solution though, and eventually they would have to remove it and evaluate whether his heart could pump on its own. This was the scariest time of my life. I can honestly say that I was so emotionally and mentally exhausted that I couldn't even pray or talk to God about what I was going through. I believe that God knows my heart, and I know that other people were actively praying for my father and my whole family. I was just trying to get through the day; we all were.

During this terrifying time, there were three separate occasions when the doctors told us it was time to say goodbye. Obviously, each of those times was devastating. We grappled with their advice to take him off of life support, but each time, he would demonstrate some small measure of progress that prevented us from doing so. The whole ordeal was such a roller coaster of emotions. It also tapped directly into one of my own worst fears: losing one of my parents. We all know that our parents are going to die, but I wasn't even close to ready (who ever is?). I am so close to both of my parents, and I know how blessed I've been to have them.

Finally, the day approached when the doctors were going to attempt to remove the balloon from my dad's heart. He was hooked up to machines that kept his lungs and kidneys functioning as well, which had shut down. Over the course of several days, the doctors began to shut off all of the machines that had been keeping my dad alive for weeks. Thank God, his organs began to work on their own again, and my father survived this harrowing health crisis. He's had a long road since then, but he's alive, which really is the most important thing.

My father's heart attack and subsequent prolonged coma was

a huge wake-up call for the whole family. We all had to take a hard look at the health choices we had been making and decide to take better care of ourselves. I had always struggled with my weight, but after this experience, I knew I had to get serious about creating a legacy like my dad's for my own children. He had made such a big impact on so many people's lives, and I want to do the same.

When my dad got sick, the inevitability of his eventual passing became so much more of a reality. Now, I'm much more intentional in my communication with him and make it a priority to involve him in my kids' lives. My dad will never be back to 100 percent health because he had some residual effects from being in the hospital, but he is doing really well. We are beyond grateful that he's still walking the journey with us.

LIVING WITH INTENTION

Being intentional about the choices I make in my life has been instrumental in actually accomplishing the things I'd like to achieve. I make a lot of lists in my life, and this area is no different. I have lists of professional goals, health goals, things I'd like to do with my wife, places we'd like to visit together, things I want to teach my kids, and lessons I find valuable. The lists are all encompassing. Like journaling, my lists help me visualize what I want to do, and I see them as the first step to getting there.

In my work, I talk with so many people who are just trying to survive the day. Life is just happening for them instead of people happening to life. Living with intention means making a choice and a decision. This can manifest itself in a myriad of ways, but for example, parents need to be intentional about how they raise their children. What values and behaviors would you like to see your children live by and exhibit? These are learned, not by accident, but by design. Making a plan for your life, or your children's lives, doesn't mean that you've mapped out every single day but rather that you have given the matter some thought, and you have a clear idea of how you would like things to go.

It's easy to get lost in the day-to-day. Everyone has pressures and fears and most of us face tragedies in one form or another. These things cannot define us or our lives. We decide how they affect us. Living intentionally means having the power to make those kinds of decisions and choosing to use that power. You choose whether or not someone makes you sad or angry or frustrated. How much power are you giving away to other people?

As a public figure, there are plenty of people who don't like me or some of the things that I say in sermons. On the flip side, there are a good number of people who do like what I say and stand for. I have to make a choice about whom I listen to and how I let it affect me. Early on, the naysayers got me down, but over time, I learned to take the power back for myself and not allow them to dictate how I feel about myself. I'm not saying this is an easy exercise by any stretch, but it is something that everyone has the power to control.

When someone or something is having a negative impact on you, give yourself permission to step away and look at it objectively. What has happened? What was said? Why is it affecting you? How could you do things differently next time? This act of slowing down and looking at things differently, rather than just reacting, is a process that takes practice.

One aspect of my life that has blossomed recently is my chance to play music. I'll never be a multiplatinum selling artist, but I absolutely love playing music. It's something I put off for a long time too because I was afraid of how people would respond. I was invited to be a part of a band in town, and initially, I turned the offer down. I had done some singing and played the saxophone in a band when I was in my 20s, but now that I was in my 30s with a plate full of responsibilities, being in a band seemed like a bad decision. I was sure there were plenty of people better at it than me.

I rationalized that I had too much going on already to fit something like playing in a band into my life. I work full time at a church, I'm a health coach, and I have a wife and two kids. Does this sound at all familiar?

I went to one of the band's shows, and as soon as I heard them, I realized immediately that I wanted to be a part of what they were doing. I sat down and talked to Lory about it. I wasn't sure what the time commitment would be or how much the band would take me away from home, but I knew I wanted to play with them. There were a million reasons to walk away, but I'm so grateful that I didn't. Playing in the band gives our fans and me so much joy. We play funk and soul songs from the '60s and '70s. We cover James Brown, Aretha Franklin, The Jackson 5, Earth, Wind, and Fire, the Ohio Players, and many more. Throngs of people come to see us whenever we play, and it's the most rewarding and energizing experience. Being in a band like this has always been a dream of mine. Now, I'm living it and loving it every step of the way. I know it is only for a season, but I am enjoying it while I can.

Another area of my life that has been positively impacted by living with intention is my weight. As I've shared, my weight has always been an issue. It's fluctuated pretty wildly throughout my life. When my father and my family were going through his heart scare, I weighed around 250 pounds. It took a couple of months after my dad's recovery (okay, maybe eight months) to get myself on board with a new health regime. Lory and I talked about it, and even though she is not overweight at all, she agreed to walk a healthier path with me.

I found a revolutionary health program that wound up changing my life. I took the health initiative very seriously and was quite strict with myself about it. The results were more than worth the strain it took to get there. In a little over four months, I lost 75 pounds. The impact of the weight loss on how I felt and my energy level inspired me to become a health coach to help others on their journey to better living. Honestly, I'm not one of those health coaches with six-pack abs and bulging muscles. I still struggle with my weight and likely always will, but I know what I need to do now when things feel like they are slipping beyond where I would like them to be. I know how to reset and get myself back on track. The program has given me those tools.

It doesn't help my weight loss goals that my wife is an amazing cook. I have a serious sweet tooth, and dessert is a big thing in our house. I have to be very intentional and controlled by only indulging in one small bite of dessert when I would prefer to have a whole serving.

There are tons of different programs out there, and I'm a fan of whatever works! The program I found works for me because accountability and coaching are big parts of their philosophy, and they are necessary for me. Most of the meals are already prepared and ready to go, so you don't have to put too much thought into it; I knew what my choices were in advance. I love this plan because you see results quickly, and it takes the guesswork and stress out of figuring out what and how much to eat.

Now that I'm a health coach, I've seen a couple dozen people also lose over 50 pounds each. I love being able to share a tool that works and that helps to change people's lives. I know my tool isn't the only tool. You just have to find something that gives you the results you are looking for within the time frame you have in mind. The point is there is always something right around the corner that can change your life if you just let it.

Simple things such as playing in a band and taking care of my health are all part of the bigger picture. I want to be someone who lives his life to the fullest, and I want to inspire others to do the same. I had a good friend who died of leukemia when I was in college. His name was Kenny Graham, and he was one of the happiest, most positive guys I have ever known. We were in a band together, and he was incredibly outgoing, charismatic, and a little eccentric. He made a big impression on me because I was such an introvert, and he just spread joy and laughter wherever he went. He lived bigger than anybody else. I was heart broken when he died, but I was also able to celebrate the fact that Kenny had touched so many peoples' lives. The rest of his friends and me were able to tell stories about Kenny and laugh our heads off just remembering what an amazing guy he was.

I want to be like that; I want to live life right up until the minute I die. I don't want to just "get by." I want to experience everything that God has given me in this life to experience. That means remembering the hard moments and celebrating all of the small wins along the way. I hope you choose to do so as well.

* *

ACTION STEPS FOR LIVING IN THE LIGHT:

1. Choose life over fear.
2. Be intentional in every aspect of your life.
3. Understand that fears can be managed, if not necessarily overcome.

CONCLUSION

"I learned that courage is not the absence of fear but the triumph over it. The bravest man is not he who does not feel afraid, but it's he who conquers that fear."

— NELSON MANDELA

My hope is that anyone who has read this far into the book is now willing to take one small baby step toward living a fuller and richer life. Fear does not have to be powerful enough to hold us back completely. We are in control, and we decide how much power fear has over our lives. One small step leads to the next small step and the next and the next.

People talk about looking at the big picture. In some circumstances, that can be the right vantage point, but when you're dealing with a fear, the smaller you can break it down, the better. Life is not about the end game; it's about the journey. If you can take life's challenges minute by minute, then hour by hour, and ultimately day by day, the likelihood that you'll enjoy the ride increases exponentially.

The first step is to find the starting gate. What does the beginning of your journey through fear and faith look like? How will you begin? When you can name your fear and recognize what it is doing in your life, you have started the process. Build your community and gather people around you who will help you move forward.

Set yourself up for success by having a winning attitude. Don't listen to those little voices in your head telling you that you can't, that your fear is too big, or that your faith is not strong enough. Having fear does not mean that your faith has failed. Get that out of your mind right now. Faith is trusting in things that we are unsure about. Get past yourself. Nothing is preventing you from living the life you want to live once you learn to silence the fear talk.

1. Start.
2. Name it.
3. Write it down.
4. Make a list.
5. Do one small thing.
6. Fuel your faith, not your fear.
7. Live the life you were meant to live.

Start small and start today. Don't wait until tomorrow; your life is waiting.

AUTHOR EDUCATION AND INSPIRATION

The desire to be in the ministry stayed with me ever since I first met Dr. Drexel Brunson in Fort Bragg, North Carolina when I was 12 years old. It felt like it something I was simply destined to do. But when it was time to go off to college, I accepted a scholarship for music at Columbus State University. I had always been told that preachers don't make a lot of money, so I felt like I needed a back-up plan. I knew I wanted to have a family one day, and I was worried about how I would support them on a minister's salary. Pretty quickly, however, I knew the music degree wasn't the right path for me. My heart wasn't in it. I had to take some time off to regroup and reassess.

There was a church in Columbus, Georgia called Cascade Hills, which opened an extension center for a seminary out of Atlanta. The pastor at Cascade Hills also had a huge heart like Dr. Brunson, and I was drawn to the seminary, even though I was still pursuing the music degree. I was at a crossroads because I had taken several online classes in Old and New Testament services and Bible study. I actually wound up with an associate degree in general science from Georgia Military College and realized I needed to stay focused in the pursuit of a college degree. After some soul searching, it dawned on me that a minister's salary would have to be enough. I knew joy would be found in what I was doing, not what I was making. Plus, there was the undeniable bonus of pursuing what I felt God was calling me to do.

Ultimately, I finished my core classes at Columbus State, transferred to Luther Rice, and earned a BA in General Ministry. From there, I went on to earn a master's of art in ministry, a master's in divinity, and a doctorate of divinity all through Luther Rice University and Seminary. My coursework was completed through a combination of online classes and in-person course work with a year off in between. Luther Rice is known as a school for the working pastor because they allow flexible modules, but it still requires a tremendous amount of focus and self-discipline. I am a big procrastinator, so the school forced me to develop some healthy habits to reduce stress.

I knew that if I wanted to make it through my doctorate degree, I needed to push on without any more breaks. It's so easy to get derailed, and I found it was harder to get back in the groove after time off. Plus, by the time I was pursuing my doctorate degree, I was married to Lory, and we wanted to start a family. I still have plans, one day, to go back and get a master's in counseling, but we'll have to see when I'll be able to find the time to do that.

Until that day, however, I will continue down the path of self-learning. I take an online class two to three times a year and read constantly. I meet with a group every Wednesday, and we talk about various aspects of leadership. It all goes back to living intentionally. I am focused on being a stronger and better leader, and I know I need to keep learning and growing to do so. I live and die by my calendar, and I schedule in time to read and learn like I would any other appointment. I don't just hope I can fit it in during the day. In the same way, I don't just hope I'll have time to spend with my wife and kids. I have to make sure that everything is scheduled so that it gets done, and that's the system that works best for me.

I follow and am inspired by other people who have found their calling in life. They help to keep me grounded and focused, and I find it relaxing to read the works of others. Many of them are in leadership positions or have been at one point or another. This means they are adept at not only guiding others but also at being the masters of their own lives, something we all try to do. I love to see people living their lives to the fullest and doing what they love to do.

Growing up, I never saw myself as a leader. I thought leaders were born with the qualities, characteristics, and intuition to be great leaders; it never occurred to me until much later that you learn how to be a leader. People have written countless books on the subject, and it is possible to study the traits that leadership requires. Goodness knows I certainly have.

In seminary, I was initially not excited by it, but I eventually came to love a book by Rusty Ricketson called *Follower First*.

He was a professor of leadership at Luther Rice, and his whole concept is built around the idea that if you want to be a good leader, you first have to be a good follower. The idea makes sense because if you're ever going to know the heart of the people and what they need from leadership, you first need to be one of them.

I find a lot of inspiration in books. Jon Acuff and Michael Hyatt are two of my favorite authors. Hyatt in particular is very interesting to me. He's a Christian, but his message has nothing to do with religion. His website and blogs are all about intentional leadership, and even though his emphasis is on leadership, he also talks about living intentionally, which is something I try to do. He offers guidance on how to lead a better life and how to be happier. It doesn't have anything to do with making money; it is focused on finding what you love to do and doing it.

I'm also influenced by Mark Batterson and Francis Chan. Both are preachers and authors, and their sermons and books hold a lot of power for me.

John Maxwell is someone I've been reading for years, and his book *Intentional Living* made an impact in my life. I like the way he communicates his ideas.

I reach out to Dr. Bill Purvis, the pastor at Cascade Hills in Columbus, Georgia, from time to time. He's had a fascinating life and has been with the same church for over 30 years, which started when there were only 18 people in the congregation. Now there are over 8,000 members! His newest book is called *Make a Break For It* and is a must-read.

It is my desire that you find freedom and live the life God created for you to live.

ABOUT THE AUTHOR

DR. NICHOLAS WILLIAMS is an author and pastor who has dedicated his life to sharing the gospel of Jesus Christ.

As a young child, Pastor Williams witnessed a horrific plane crash that had a profound impact on him, resulting in not only a deep and paralyzing fear of flying, but a cautious approach to life in general. Decades later, he began to realize that his fears were holding him back, and after years of work managed to overcome those fears and find true confidence and happiness. Through his work, Pastor Williams now helps others to confront and defeat their fears.

Pastor Williams received his B.A., M.A.M., M.Div., and D.Min. from Luther Rice University. He lives in Sarasota, Florida, with his wife Lory and their two children, Aubrie and Noah. You can find out more about him at nicwilliams.me.

Made in the USA
San Bernardino, CA
23 June 2016